Creative CBT Interventions
for
Children with Anxiety

Liana Lowenstein

Champion Press
Toronto

Library and Archives Canada Cataloguing in Publication

Lowenstein, Liana, 1965– author
    Creative CBT interventions for children with anxiety / Liana Lowenstein.

Includes bibliographical references.
ISBN 978-0-9951725-0-0 (paperback)

    1. Anxiety in children--Treatment. 2. Anxiety disorders--Treatment.
3. Cognitive therapy for children. 4. Child psychotherapy. I. Title.

RJ506.A58L68 2016   618.92'8522   C2016-904505-6

Correspondence regarding this book can be sent to:
Champion Press
PO Box 91012, 2901 Bayview Avenue, Toronto, Ontario, Canada M2K 2Y6
Telephone: (416) 575-7836
Email: info@lianalowenstein.com
Website: www.lianalowenstein.com

About the Author

Liana Lowenstein, MSW, is a Registered Social Worker, Certified TF-CBT Therapist, and Certified Play Therapist-Supervisor who has worked with children and their families since 1988. In addition to her clinical practice in Toronto, she provides consultation to mental health agencies, runs a Play Therapy Internship Program, and speaks at agency training events and conferences locally and internationally. She served on the board of directors of the Canadian Association for Child and Play Therapy for nine years and is the former Education Chair of the Canadian Play Therapy Certificate Program. She is the founder of Champion Press Publishing Company and is the author of *Creative Interventions for Troubled Children & Youth; Creative Interventions for Bereaved Children; Cory Helps Kids Cope with Divorce; Cory Helps Kids Cope with Sexual Abuse,* and other acclaimed books on child and family therapy. She is the winner of the Monica Herbert Award for outstanding contribution and dedication to child psychotherapy and play therapy in Canada.

Also by Liana Lowenstein

Paper Dolls and Paper Airplanes:
Therapeutic Exercises for Sexually Traumatized Children
(co-authored with Geraldine Crisci & Marilyn Lay)

Creative Interventions for Troubled Children & Youth

More Creative Interventions for Troubled Children & Youth

Creative Interventions for Bereaved Children

Creative Interventions for Children of Divorce

Assessment and Treatment Techniques for Children, Adolescents,
and Families: Practitioners Share Their Most Effective Techniques
(Volumes One through Three)

Creative Family Therapy Techniques:
Play, Art, and Expressive Therapies to Engage
Children in Family Sessions

Cory Helps Kids Cope with Divorce:
Playful Therapeutic Activities for Young Children

Cory Helps Kids Cope with Sexual Abuse:
Playful Activities for Traumatized Children

For more information on the above books and forthcoming
publications, visit the author's website:
www.lianalowenstein.com

Contents

Activities at a Glance

ACTIVITY	OBJECTIVE	AGES	MODALITY
Welcome Letter	Explain process of therapy, confidentiality	8–12	I
Jamie's Story: Getting Help	Explain therapist's role, increase comfort with therapist	5–8	I
How About You?	Articulate increased comfort with therapist	6–12	I, G, F
Five Favorites	Articulate increased comfort with therapist	6–12	I
Sticky Dots	Identify fears, worries, and other concerns	6–14	I
Butterflies in My Stomach	Identify fears and worries	6–12	I
Red and Black Card Game	Articulate feelings, cognitions, physiological symptoms	8–12	I
People in My World	Articulate perception of significant relationships	6–12	I
Jamie's Story: Anxiety	Explain anxiety, physiological responses, CBT	6–8	I
Crumpled Paper Throw	Explain anxiety, physiological responses, CBT	8–12	I, G, F
Close Far Game	Identify body changes indicative of anxiety and stress	6–10	I, G, F
Cookie Breathing Game	Apply diaphragmatic breathing to decrease anxiety	6–10	I, G, F
Awesome App	Apply diaphragmatic breathing to decrease anxiety	10-16	I
Tight-Relax Game	Apply muscle relaxation to decrease anxiety	6–8	I
Jamie's Story: Feelings	Verbally articulate emotions and their intensity	5–8	I
Guess Which Hand	Verbally articulate emotions and their intensity	6–10	I, F
Air Hockey Feelings Game	Verbally articulate emotions and their intensity	8–12	I, F
Letting Butterflies Out of Bag	Structure and limit pervasive worry	6–12	I, P
Jamie's Story: Helpful Thoughts	Replace unhelpful thoughts with helpful thoughts	6–8	I
Helpful Thoughts	Replace unhelpful thoughts with helpful thoughts	8–14	I, G, F
Bug Off!	Replace unhelpful thoughts with helpful thoughts	8–12	I
Willy's Worries & Wise Wizard	Replace negative self-talk with positive self-talk	8–12	I, G
Jamie's Story: Facing Fears	Explain rationale of and readiness for gradual exposure	6–10	I
Picture It Poster	Face feared situation with minimal anxiety	6–12	I
Play Clay Role-Play	Articulate readiness to face feared situation	6–9	I, F
Best Friend Role-Play	Articulate readiness to face feared situation	9–14	I, F
Brag Book (Child Version)	Increase child's positive view of self	6–12	P
Brag Book (Parent Version)	Increase positive parenting practices	N/A	P
Table Talk	Increase communication between child and parent	6–16	P
Reward Bag	Increase child's positive behavior	6–12	P
Play Date	Increase pleasurable time between parent and child	6–12	F
Success Story	Verbalize ability to manage challenges	6–16	P
Cookie Jar	Articulate why, when, and how therapy will end	6–10	I, G, F
Balloon Bash	Review and articulate concepts learned in therapy	6–8	I
Crumpled Paper Throw: Sequel	Review and articulate concepts learned in therapy	8–12	I, G, F
Coping with Anxiety Game	Identify the need for continued use of CBT strategies	8–12	I, G, F

Modality: I = Individual Therapy, G = Group Therapy, F = Family Therapy, P = Parent Session

Acknowledgments

My heartfelt thanks are due first to the courageous children and parents I have worked with over the years, who taught me so much about the determination and resilience of the human spirit to overcome obstacles. They are the true inspiration for this book.

I owe a tremendous debt of gratitude to Aureen Wagner, Athena Drewes, Khush Amaria, Jessica Cooperman, Sheri Eggleton, and Leanne Matlow, who so generously donated their time to review the manuscript, providing me with valuable insight and suggestions. I am very grateful to the many colleagues who graciously took the time to try the activities with their clients, and who offered helpful feedback. Special thanks goes to Susan Knell and Paris Goodyear Brown for their supportive words. Much appreciation goes to Linda Pruessen for her editorial assistance, and to Kim Bracic for her design work.

Special gratitude is expressed to my family for their continued support and encouragement. I am especially thankful to my husband, Steven, and my daughter, Jaime, for their love and for their amazing patience as I spent hours in front of my computer working on this book.

Introduction

This book provides mental health practitioners with creative interventions to engage, assess, and treat children with anxiety. The activities are geared to children aged 6 through 12, but many can be modified for both younger and older clients. Although the book is focused on treating childhood anxiety, some of the interventions can be used with other treatment populations. For example, many clients would respond well to activities from the sections on Engagement, Relaxation, Affective Expression, and Parenting Skills.

Treatment Approach

The activities in this book are based on cognitive behavioral therapy (CBT), which is a highly effective model for treating childhood anxiety. A thorough explanation of the theory and process of CBT for childhood anxiety is beyond the scope of this text. It is therefore essential that mental health practitioners using this book be well grounded in the theory and practice of CBT in general, as well as in its application to the treatment of childhood anxiety. Suggestions for additional reading can be found in the "References and Suggested Readings" section. A list of organizations that provide relevant training is also included at the end of this book.

The interventions contained herein address the key components of CBT for childhood anxiety; namely, psychoeducation, relaxation skills, affective expression, cognitive coping, exposure, and parent training. These components are presented in a particular sequence and are meant to be followed in order, with the exception of the interventions for parent sessions, which can be integrated throughout the treatment process.

A variety of activities are presented within each chapter so the practitioner can select interventions most appropriate to their client's age, interests, and needs. Additional interventions from other sources can be integrated into the child's treatment as needed.

Comprehensive treatment of childhood anxiety has the greatest chance of success when it utilizes a multimodal approach (Connolly & Bernstein, 2007). This includes collaboration with the child's school, such as gathering information from the child's teacher (see Appendix A) and providing information on ways the school can support the child (see Appendix B).

In addition to CBT, some children benefit from medication prescribed and monitored by a pediatrician/child psychiatrist. Social skills training and increased social opportunities are essential additional components for children diagnosed with social anxiety disorder (Spence et al., 2000). CBT for specific phobia focuses on exposure and includes cognitive modification of unrealistic fears and participant modeling (Berman et al., 2000; Velting et al., 2004). Modifications of standard CBT for anxiety are required for selective mutism and panic disorder.

Anxiety disorders in children are often comorbid with other psychiatric disorders including depression, attention-deficit/hyperactivity disorder, oppositional defiant disorder, and learning disorders (Manassis, 2009). Comorbid disorders should be assessed and, when needed, treated separately or concurrently with the anxiety disorder. This is well described in Manassis (2009).

If the child's parents are highly anxious, or if there are concerns related to family dysfunction, these issues need to be addressed prior to or concurrently with CBT. Parent behaviors that undermine the effectiveness of CBT (e.g., not bringing the child consistently to sessions, difficulty encouraging the child's progress, and failing to follow through with at-home practicing exercises) will need to be problem-solved. Helpful ideas can be found in Killough-McGuire and McGuire (2001) and Manassis (2009).

This book provides practitioners with child-friendly CBT techniques that can facilitate their clinical work with young clients. Practitioners must use therapeutic techniques in a clinically and theoretically sound manner, and pay special attention to the process underlying each technique. Attending to the process of CBT with anxious children "is essential and ensures that the theoretical model and the core principles that underpin it are at the forefront of the Clinician's thinking" (Stallard, 2005, p. 2). The use of clinical supervision (peer, private, agency supplied) is highly recommended when implementing new therapeutic techniques.

Playful Interventions

Creative, play-based activities, presented within the context of an empathically attuned therapeutic relationship, engage children and enhance the effectiveness of CBT. Blending structured play techniques with CBT allows for effective implementation of CBT while retaining its theoretical underpinnings. Play has a critical role in CBT with children, as it provides an accessible, developmentally appropriate context for children to participate in therapy (Knell & Dasari, 2011; Podell et al., 2009; Shelby & Berk, 2009). The therapist's ability to be creative, reduce focus on verbalizations, and increase use of playful experiential approaches can contribute to the successful adaptation of CBT with children (Drewes, 2009; Knell 1993; Knell & Dasari, 2006, 2011).

The therapeutic rapport with children "is as important in CBT as in any other treatment modality, and the therapist can be creative and playful to promote child engagement in treatment" (Pincus et al., 2011, p. 222). Pleasurable, playful activities are "known to lower levels of stress chemicals, enabling children to deal more successfully with stressful situations" (Plummer, 2012, p. 30). When children are engaged in games and playful activities, they are not only having fun but they are also relaxing and learning new skills.

Play in itself is therapeutic and becomes a change agent and therapeutic power when used within treatment (Schaefer & Drewes, 2013). Furthermore, "in order to obviate the possibility that CBT is dull and boring to children, it is incumbent upon cognitive behavioral therapists to develop creative and engaging ways to deliver these skills to children" (Friedberg et al., 2000, p. 190). Developmentally appropriate and fun hands-on activities have a more positive impact as children understand them, enjoy them, and are more motivated to participate (Friedberg & McClure, 2015).

Parental Involvement and Homework

Parental support and involvement in treatment is a key factor to the child's optimal success in therapy. Separate sessions with parents as well as conjoint sessions should be conducted as part of the overall treatment plan. Engagement with the parents is essential to avoid premature termination of treatment.

This book includes information sheets to be given to the parents. They summarize key points and provide tips so parents can better support their child. There are several options regarding how to integrate these information sheets into the treatment process. One option is to give them to the parents to read between sessions, and then to review them during the parent sessions. Another option is to review them during the parent sessions and then give them to the parents at the end of the session to enhance the learning between sessions. These information sheets are not intended to replace face-to-face therapy sessions or contact with the parents. Rather, they were developed to provide supplemental information to parents on key issues, and as tools to guide the focus of the parent sessions.

Skill-building is an important component of CBT. Assigning home-based practice exercises is one way to facilitate generalization and mastery of skills learned in sessions. The home-based practice exercises must be easy to understand, realistically accomplished, relevant to the client's treatment needs, psychologically meaningful, and engaging.

Homework (practice) activities are given at the end of sessions, ideally with child and parent both present. Reviewing the practice exercise and possibly starting it in session facilitates compliance at home. Potential obstacles for completing the task at home should be explored (e.g., "What might get in the way of you doing this task at home?"). It is also helpful to discuss ways the task can help the client (e.g., "How do you think this will be helpful to you?") (Friedberg & McClure, 2015, p. 203). Practitioners (or parents) may wish to offer a small reward for completing home-based practice exercises to encourage motivation (see the Reward Bag in the "Parenting Skills" section).

Some children avoid doing the home-based practice task because it is anxiety-provoking. Since noncompliance is a function of the child's presenting problem of anxiety, helping the child "identify and modify thoughts and feelings surrounding the task becomes a central therapeutic issue" (Friedberg & McClure, 2015, p. 208). Following up on home-based practice exercises at the start of the next session is essential and reinforces its importance.

Praising parents for their motivation in treatment is important in therapy, just as it is with child clients. Parents benefit from positive reinforcement from the practitioner, especially when therapeutic progress is made and when they follow through with coaching their child to practice and utilize CBT strategies at home. Some parents may inadvertently enable their child's anxiety and should therefore be commended by the practitioner when they appropriately support their child.

Working with Challenging Children

Working with difficult-to-engage clients can be frustrating and challenging, even for seasoned clinicians. The challenge of working with children in therapy can be further compounded by their fear of entering therapy, their lack of control over the decision to attend therapy, their feeling of being scapegoated for family problems, their lack of motivation for treatment, and their developmental capacity, which can make it difficult for them to respond to traditional talk-therapy. Children who are oppositional or extremely withdrawn can be particularly difficult to engage in therapy.

At times, lack of engagement in therapy can be attributed to a poor therapeutic alliance. Common factors that may undermine a positive therapeutic rapport include ambivalence about therapy, shifting intensity of symptoms, unexpected crises in the life of the child and family, poor match between therapist and client, difficulty forming a trusting relationship, and transference or countertransference (Manassis, 2009). Resistance in sessions may also stem from the client's feeling that therapy is too much like schoolwork and, therefore, not engaging.

The first step in working with hard-to-engage clients is understanding the reasons underlying their clinical presentation. A different approach will be needed depending on the factors at play. When working with extremely withdrawn children, for example, it is first important to complete a thorough assessment, as working with depressive withdrawal is different than working with anxious withdrawal. Manassis (2009) offers a number of helpful tips for working with withdrawn children, including reinforcing every minor sign of engagement (such as eye contact with the practitioner), utilizing a playful approach that de-emphasizes the need to respond verbally, making it clear that there are no "wrong" answers, and increasing the involvement of parents.

Children with both an internalizing and externalizing disorder (such as anxiety and attention-deficit/hyperactivity disorder) may benefit from a combination of medication and behavior modification prior to addressing internalizing problems via CBT (Manassis, 2009). Clear and consistent limits, redirecting techniques, frequent and desirable rewards, and the minimizing of distractions are helpful approaches with inattentive children. Short, active, engaging therapeutic activities are more appropriate for this client population.

Building treatment readiness is an essential element to engaging children in therapy. Optimal therapeutic progress is likely to be increased when the child and family are properly prepared and ready for treatment. Readiness for treatment entails "the ability to channel the desire to get well into the action to get well" (Wagner, 2005, p. 104). Building treatment readiness involves a four-step process: stabilization, communication, persuasion, and collaboration. These steps are elaborated on in detail in Wagner's book (2005).

Tips and Clinical Guidelines

The therapeutic value of the activities in this book rests largely on the practitioner's skill, abilities, and demeanor. Practitioners must therefore have proper training and expertise in CBT with childhood anxiety and a warm and engaging manner with clients. Below are additional guidelines for appropriately using this book:

- Select and modify the clinical activities to suit the developmental, cultural, and clinical needs of the child. **If adaptations are made to any of the activities, be sure to maintain the following copyright notice on every page: © Original copyright Liana Lowenstein 2016. All rights reserved.).**

- Gather required materials prior to each session, and copy activities and parent information sheets for the clients. **(The activities in this book may be reproduced by the individual purchaser for direct use with clients in a therapeutic setting. Any other use or reproduction is a violation of international copyright laws.)**

-   The activities in this book have been written in a way that allows the practitioner to read the instructions directly to the child, regardless of their age and reading ability. This will ensure that the instructions are clearly heard.

-   Give the child a scrapbook (or binder) in the first session in which to place activities completed during sessions. The scrapbook has several benefits: it allows the child to see the progression of sessions; it provides immediate tangible reinforcement of each therapeutic success; and it gives the child a lasting record once therapy is terminated. The scrapbook should be kept in a locked place in the practitioner's office. It can be given to the child in the last session, with a discussion regarding who, if anyone, should see it, and where in the child's home it should be kept to ensure its privacy.

-   Follow the same structure in every session to enable the client to become comfortable with the predictability of the therapeutic process. Begin each session with a brief check-in activity (for examples, see the video titled Rapport-Building and Check-In Activities on the author's YouTube channel: http://www.youtube.com/user/lowensteinliana). Next, complete the planned activity. Review skills learned and discuss the implementation of the home-based practice task. Devote the last part of the session to child-led play or to a fun activity.

-   Introduce interventions using an enthusiastic tone, carefully process by using exploratory questions and facilitative responses, and bring appropriate closure before moving on to the next task or activity.

-   Consider giving small rewards to facilitate engagement and motivation. For example, the child can earn points or tokens, then trade those in for a prize from the goodie box once ten points or tokens have been earned (see the Points Tracking Sheet in Appendix C). Or the child can earn Lego or beads and make something once enough have been accumulated. (It can be helpful to provide the child with a resealable plastic bag labeled with the child's name to hold the tokens, Lego, or beads.)

-   Be sensitive to the pacing of the therapy, and consider slowing down the process if the child becomes overly resistant, anxious, or dysregulated.

-   Schedule periodic review meetings with the clients to discuss goals achieved, problem-solve any barriers to treatment, and ensure they continue to perceive sessions as helpful and relevant. The Therapy Feedback Form in Appendix D can be used midway through therapy as a means to explore these issues with clients.

-   Prepare the client well in advance for termination. Clearly explain to the parent and child how and when therapy will end. Creating and regularly reviewing a treatment plan helps to inform the child, parent, and therapist when goals have been achieved and the client is ready for the termination phase of therapy. The Cookie Jar activity (see Section 9: Termination) prepares younger clients for the ending of therapy. Introduce this activity when there are five sessions remaining.

The activities in this book have been specifically designed to capture and sustain children's interest in and motivation for therapy, and to help them address anxiety within the context of a safe and playful therapeutic environment. By freeing children from the distress caused by anxiety, practitioners can make an enormous difference in their lives.

Section 1

Initial Meeting with Parents

Doing cognitive behavioral therapy (CBT) with children necessitates the active participation of parents. It is recommended that the child's parents be interviewed, preferably together, prior to the first meeting with the child. The first face-to-face session with the parents is critical, as it sets the tone for ongoing work. The focus of this initial session is on (1) developing a therapeutic rapport; (2) establishing the need for mental health intervention; (3) discussing prior therapy experiences; (4) augmenting the parents' motivation for treatment; (5) encouraging the parents' involvement in therapy; (6) establishing a collaborative working relationship; and (7) gathering relevant information (McKay et al., 2004). Killough McGuire and McGuire (2001) outline strategies that can be undertaken to engage parents:

- Be respectful at all times, even in the face of parental anger and hostility.

- Truly listen to parents as they vent about their stressors and frustrations, and reflect, validate, and empathize with their feelings.

- Give time and attention to the agenda and treatment goals of the parents and paraphrase so they feel heard.

- Point out the strengths of the parents, especially their concern for the child.

- Explore the parents' potential concerns related to differences of culture, gender, religion, or other factors that may make them feel they are not being understood, accepted, or respected.

- Discuss and try to resolve practical barriers to participating in treatment (e.g., lack of transportation, scheduling conflicts, and lack of childcare).

A questionnaire and an information sheet for parents are included in this section to aid in the engagement and assessment process. The information on the questionnaire should be collected via a face-to-face interview. This facilitates rapport-building, and allows the practitioner to elicit more detailed information than would otherwise be obtained if the parents were to complete it on their own. The practitioner needs to be cognizant of the fact that gathering detailed information regarding presenting issues and concerns can be a sensitive issue. For this reason, the practitioner must convey empathy and validate feelings during the information gathering process. Moreover, parents of anxious children are often highly anxious themselves, so the practitioner should be mindful of the parents' feelings of nervousness, and take care to assess their mental health issues.

The Information Sheet for Parents can be reviewed in the initial session. It provides a brief explanation of CBT and its effectiveness, and presents the rationale for a playful therapeutic approach. It outlines ways the parents can help make therapy a positive experience.

In order for clients to engage in therapy, they must perceive it as "relevant, valuable, and capable of achieving desired goals and outcomes" (Springer & Misurell, 2015, p. 25). Thus, in the initial session with parents, the opportunity exists for the practitioner to convey the benefits of therapy. As therapy progresses, periodic discussions with clients should focus on reviewing goals achieved and ensuring that the clients continue to perceive the sessions as helpful and relevant. The Therapy Feedback Form in Appendix D can be used midway through therapy as a means to explore these issues with clients.

Children want to progress in therapy, but they often fail to recognize that dealing with anxiety "is usually an inconsistent pattern involving surges in progress and regressions to old habits" (Foxman, 2004, p. 212). Conveying this to clients is normalizing and helps to manage treatment expectations.

PARENT QUESTIONNAIRE

Child's Name: _____ **Date of Birth:**_____ **Age:**_____

Child's Address: _____

Child's Placement (with whom does the child live?):

___ Both Biological Parents ___ Biological Mother ___ Biological Father ___ Step Parent

___ Adoptive Parent ___ Foster /Kinship Care ___ Shelter ___ Other (Specify) _____

Who has legal custody of the child? _____(provide copy of custody order for the file)

Mother's Name: _____ **Date of Birth:** _____ **Place of Birth:** _____

Mother's Address: _____ **Mother's Email:** _____

Mother's Phone (H): _____ **(W):** _____ **(C):** _____

Mother's Educational Background, Occupation: _____**Work Hours:** _____

Fathers's Name: _____ **Date of Birth:** _____ **Place of Birth:** _____

Father's Address: _____ **Father's Email:** _____

Father's Phone (H): _____ **(W):** _____ **(C):** _____

Father's Educational Background, Occupation: _____**Work Hours:** _____

Child's School: _____ **Teacher:** _____ **Grade:** _____ **Phone#:** _____

List all those living in your child's home:

Name	Relationship	Age/School/Occupation
_____	_____	_____
_____	_____	_____
_____	_____	_____
_____	_____	_____
_____	_____	_____

List other persons closely involved with your child but not living in the home, and describe their roles:

_____

_____

_____

_____

What are your concerns about your child that made you seek therapy at this time?

_____

_____

_____

Describe your child as an infant/toddler (list any complications at birth, delays in development, general difficulties, signs of excessive worry, or fears):

_____

_____

_____

_____

_____

_____

Describe any serious life stresses your child has experienced (such as placement away from home, physical or sexual abuse, neglect, domestic violence, divorce, other stressful or frightening events):

_____

_____

_____

_____

_____

List hospitalizations, serious health issues/allergies, any ongoing medications your child is taking:

_____

_____

_____

_____

Describe concerns raised by daycare/school about your child (behavioral, peer, academic):

_____

_____

Describe concerns related to your child's expression of anger (tantrums, physically aggressive, hurts self):

_____

_____

Describe concerns related to daily routines (doesn't follow routines or stay on task, poor organizational skills):

_____

_____

Describe concerns related to peers (doesn't have many friends, very shy, gets teased, aggressive with peers):

_____

_____

Describe prior assessment/therapy your child received (name of professional, dates, diagnosis, nature of interventions). Describe what you found least/most helpful about prior therapy:

_____

_____

What are your child's strengths, interests? List any after-school activities your child regularly attends:

_____

_____

Describe your relationship with your child, and your strengths and weaknesses as a parent:

_____

_____

Who disciplines the child and how is the child disciplined? List some parenting strategies you find helpful:

_____

_____

_____

_____

What situations, people, places make your child's anxiety worse? Better?

_____

_____

How does your child typically deal with fearful situations (e.g., avoids, cries, yells, clings, seeks reassurance)?

_____

_____

How does your child's anxiety impact your family's day-to-day functioning (e.g., has your family changed routines to accommodate your child's anxiety)?

_____

_____

Describe a time you responded in a way that reduced your child's anxiety (including why your child was anxious, and what you said/did):

_____

_____

Describe a time you felt you could have handled your child's anxiety better (including why your child was anxious, and what you said/did):

_____

_____

Are there any issues or problems that might make it difficult for you/your child to attend sessions (e.g., transportation, childcare, appointment times, fees)? If yes, please explain:

_____

_____

What would need to happen for you to feel like therapy was worthwhile?

_____

_____

_____

_____

_____

Parent/Caregiver's Background (make copies for each parent/caregiver to complete):

Where were you raised and by whom? Describe past/current relationship with your parents:

_____

_____

_____

List brothers and sisters, their ages, whereabouts, current relationship you have:

_____

_____

_____

Describe any serious life stresses you experienced during childhood and how it affected you (such as physical or sexual abuse, neglect, abandonment, divorce, witnessed spousal abuse, other trauma):

_____

_____

_____

_____

_____

_____

_____

_____

_____

_____

Describe the happiest time/experience you recall from your childhood:

_____

_____

_____

Describe the saddest time/experience you recall from your childhood:

_____

_____

_____

Describe if you or any relatives have ever had any of the following:

Serious illness: _____

Anxiety Disorder: _____

Obsessive-Compulsive Disorder: _____

Depression/Bipolar Disorder: _____

Learning Disability: _____

Attention-Deficit Hyperactivity Disorder: _____

Eating Disorder: _____

Alcoholism/drug abuse: _____

Other mental health concern: _____

Criminal conviction: _____

Have you been seen previously for assessment/counseling/marital counseling or are you currently in therapy? (If yes, indicate name of professional, date/place of service, for what purpose, and any diagnosis provided.)

_____

_____

_____

_____

Please add any other information about your background that you feel is important:

_____

_____

_____

_____

_____

_____

_____

_____

_____

_____

Information Sheet for Parents: Therapy for Childhood Anxiety

Key Points

- All children occasionally feel anxious. Anxiety is a problem when children feel excessively, unreasonably, and persistently anxious and it interferes with social activities, school performance, or sleep. If anxiety is adversely affecting your child's life, then your child will benefit from learning ways to manage it.

- Anxiety is very treatable, and success rates with the appropriate treatment are excellent. Cognitive behavioral therapy (CBT) is the most commonly used approach for anxious children. This is because there is a great deal of research that supports the effectiveness of CBT in the treatment of childhood anxiety. In CBT, children learn a variety of anxiety management strategies. (CBT will be discussed in further detail in future sessions.)

- Children often have difficulty talking about their issues, so play-based CBT activities are used (such as games and art) to make therapy more appealing and to motivate children to learn key skills.

- It's important to complete a thorough assessment so we can develop treatment goals geared to the unique needs of your child and family.

- Children do better in therapy when parents are active participants.

- Therapy for childhood anxiety takes time and effort. Therefore, it is important to think of the stressors you can take off your plate to better enable you to focus on therapy. If it's tough for you to do this, let's brainstorm some ideas.

- During the course of therapy, most children show signs of progress but also at times regress to old habits. This is normal and should not be perceived as treatment failure. Coaching your child to regularly use skills learned in therapy will help to sustain the gains they have made.

- Therapy is not a cure for anxiety. However, please be reassured that when children receive appropriate treatment, they learn lifelong skills so anxiety no longer rules their lives.

Tips

There are many ways you can help make therapy more beneficial for your child. Below are some ideas:

- Prepare your child for the first session (e.g., "We're going to see someone named ___ whose job is to help kids with their worries and upset feelings. She/he helps kids by talking and playing with them").

- Try not to force or bribe your child to come to therapy, or give punishments if your child refuses to come. If there is a problem bringing your child to therapy, please contact me to consult.

- Keep me informed of significant updates on your child and family so I can plan accordingly. It is best to contact me when your child is not present so concerns can be discussed freely. Please contact me well in advance of the session, rather than at the time of the appointment, so I can plan for the session and so your child can benefit from the full session time.

- Progress takes time, so do not expect immediate change. Be patient and praise your child's effort and small successes.

Section 2

Engagement and Assessment

This chapter includes techniques to engage and assess anxious children. The engagement activities precede the assessment interventions because a positive therapeutic rapport must be established prior to beginning the assessment. A safe and trusting therapeutic relationship is the key to a positive outcome in therapy (Eltz, Shirk & Sarlin, 1995; Kearney, Wechsler, Kauer & Lemos-Miller, 2010; Ormhaug, Jensen, Wentzel-Larsen & Shirk, 2013). Developing a positive rapport and establishing a safe environment for clients leads to a deeper and more significant level of sharing in sessions.

The process of engagement may be easier for practitioners who work with adults, as their clients are often already motivated and prepared to actively participate in therapy (Stallard, 2005). Careful attention therefore needs to be given to the process of engaging children in therapy.

While the engagement process goes beyond simply using a game, playful techniques help create a safe and positive therapeutic environment for children. Fun activities create an "inviting and motivating atmosphere" (Springer & Misurell, 2015, p. 27). This chapter presents several rapport-building activities. Some clients, especially highly anxious children, will need additional sessions devoted specifically to building rapport. There are a wide variety of creative engagement techniques to choose from in the literature, including Rock, Paper, Scissors (Cavett, 2010); Google It (Sousa, 2011); Ice Breaker (Kenney-Noziska, 2008); and The I Don't Know game (Lowenstein, 2002). Rapport-building games and activities provide useful strategies that can engage children, but it is the practitioner's use of self that is the most powerful engagement tool. The practitioner's warmth, consistency, patience, and unconditional acceptance of the child are the key ingredients to put children at ease and help develop a positive therapeutic rapport.

The clinical assessment is a critical component of the intervention process, as it forms the foundation for effective treatment planning. The ultimate purpose of assessing children is to offer them treatment that is as effective and efficient as possible. A comprehensive clinical assessment should be conducted for the following reasons:

- Determines whether the child needs treatment, and if so, what needs to be treated

- Enables the practitioner to tailor treatment to the child's needs

- Provides direction on best treatment modalities (e.g., individual, group, family)

- Enables the practitioner to provide accurate feedback to parents on the child's needs

Friedberg, McClure, and Garcia stress the importance of case conceptualization. They state, "case conceptualization increases the flexibility of treatment strategies, allows the therapist to recognize what techniques work and which procedures fall flat, and facilitates productive troubleshooting when treatment is stymied" (2009, p. 4).

During the assessment process, control of the pace is critical. It is important to be cognizant of non-verbal signs of discomfort if a child is reluctant to speak up. Some children may be very compliant even when they are in distress. If the child does need to take a break from an assessment activity or stop talking about a particularly distressing issue, it can be helpful to switch to an activity that fosters coping, so the child does not feel helpless. In these instances, it is important to make a statement about coming back to the activity or issue when the child feels ready. This conveys the message that avoidance of distressing events is not a healthy long-term coping strategy.

As the child is completing the assessment activity, it is important to discuss and explore the child's responses to glean additional information. Maintaining a calm and accepting manner will help the child feel supported. Normalizing, validating, and reflecting the child's feelings will reassure the child and communicate understanding.

A comprehensive assessment includes exploring the family dynamics that contribute to the child's functioning. Evaluating children within the context of their family can provide useful clinical information that assists in the development of treatment goals. Innovative and engaging family assessment activities can be found in *Creative Family Therapy Techniques: Play, Art, and Expressive Activities to Engage Children in Family Sessions* (Lowenstein, 2010b), and *Play in Family Therapy* (Gil, 2014).

Collecting information from multiple sources and across multiple environments is essential because of variable agreement among informants (Choudhury et al., 2003). Therefore, in addition to meeting with the parents and the child, information should be collected from relevant collaterals such as a teacher, previous therapist, and pediatrician. Gathering information from the child's school and working closely with school personnel is especially important given the central role school plays in the child's day-to-day life (see the Teacher Questionnaire in Appendix A and Tips for School Personnel in Appendix B).

Structured or semi-structured interviews and self-report measures designed specifically to assess anxiety in children should be incorporated into the assessment. It is important that these measures be administered by a mental health professional with appropriate licensure and training.

In addition to assessing the nature and severity of anxiety-related symptoms, it is essential to explore other issues that require therapeutic intervention.

The activities in this chapter assess the child's fears, worries, and other areas of distress; physiological responses to anxiety; family and community relationships; and coping strategies.

After the assessment has been completed, it is advisable for the practitioner to meet with the parents (and possibly the child) to provide feedback on the assessment results. The practitioner then collaborates with the clients to set and prioritize treatment goals. A strong treatment plan sets realistic, measurable goals, and is revised as needed with caregivers, the treatment team, and (if appropriate) the child.

It is imperative that information on CBT (and the research to support its effectiveness) be provided to parents so they are clear on the rationale, benefits, and key elements of the model, and so that parents might provide informed consent to proceed with treatment. It is particularly important to properly explain the process and benefits of gradual exposure and to help clients embrace this aspect of treatment. Although the critical role of parents in treatment should have been discussed in the initial parent meeting, it can be re-emphasized in the feedback session.

Engagement Interventions

Welcome Letter (page 24)
Ages: 8–12
Objective: Explain therapist's role, confidentiality, and format of sessions
Description:
When children attend therapy, they may feel confused about why they are there and nervous about what to expect. The Welcome Letter can be read to the child at the beginning of the first session to normalize feelings, clarify the practitioner's role and duty to report safety concerns, and explain the format of sessions. Modify the letter to suit the child's age and circumstances. Place the letter on the first page of the child's scrapbook.

Jamie's Story (Chapter One: Getting Help) (page 25)
Ages: 5–8
Objective: Explain therapist's role; increase comfort with therapist
Supplies: Bag filled with small prizes
Description:
Storytelling can be an effective therapeutic tool with children. Jamie's Story (Chapter One: Getting Help) facilitates rapport-building, normalizes anxiety, and explains the therapeutic process. Children will identify with Jamie, the central character in the story, and will have increased understanding and insight after reading the story. Jamie is an androgynous name, so the story can apply to any gender. Questions and reinforcers are woven throughout the story to captivate and sustain the child's interest in the content, and to evaluate and encourage the child's integration of the material. Jamie's Story is geared to younger clients. Therefore, carefully review the story to decide on its appropriateness for the client's age and developmental level.

How About You? (page 27)

Ages: 6–12
Objective: Get acquainted; establish a positive therapeutic environment
Supplies: Ball
Description:
This fun and active game helps the practitioner and client to become better acquainted and sets the tone for a playful therapeutic environment. The game facilitates bidirectional sharing and playful interaction that can be particularly helpful in the rapport-building phase. Maintain the child's interest in the game by moving it along quickly, and playing about six to eight rounds. The practitioner can obtain a clearer understanding of this activity by watching a demonstration on the author's YouTube channel: http://www.youtube.com/user/lowensteinliana.

Five Favorites (page 28)

Ages: 6–12
Objective: Get acquainted; establish a positive therapeutic environment
Supplies: Paper bag, scissors
Advance Preparation:
Cut out the five game cards (see page 28), fold each card, and place the cards in a paper bag.
Description:
Engagement begins in the first session and forms the basis for a positive therapeutic rapport. Throughout the game, the practitioner and client get to know one another by sharing non-threatening information. The game cards can be changed to other "favorites" such as favorite toy, sport, celebrity, holiday, song, book, etc. The game can be played standing up with children who have difficulty sitting and focusing.

Assessment Interventions

Sticky Dots (page 29)

Ages: 7–12
Objective: Identify and quantify areas of distress
Supplies: 1/4-inch adhesive dots (available at office supply stores)
Description:
This activity provides rich assessment information regarding the child's areas of distress, as well as the intensity of the distress. It enables children to identify their clinical issues without having to verbalize them directly, so it is particularly useful with children who have difficulty talking about their problems. The concept of scaling is explained so clients can ascribe the appropriate number of adhesive dots to each statement. Wait until the child has finished placing the self-adhesive dots for all 19 items on the worksheet before asking exploratory questions about the client's responses, so as to not affect the processing phase.

Butterflies in My Stomach (page 30)

Ages: 6–12

Objective: Identify fears and worries

Supplies: Several copies of the butterfly outlines, scissors, markers, paper bag

Advance Preparation:

Cut out the butterfly outlines.

Description:

Butterflies in My Stomach ascertains the child's specific fears and worries. It is particularly useful with children who have a multitude of fears and worries as it enables them to communicate which problems are most pressing and need priority in treatment. Comparing the child's reported fears and worries with information gleaned from parents and teachers serves as an indicator of the child's openness. If the child is reluctant to identify fears and worries, a normalizing statement can encourage disclosure: "Everyone has fears and worries. This is a list of some fears and worries that other kids have talked about. Let's look at the list to see which fears and worries bother you." The completed activity forms part of the client's assessment, and can be referred to in later sessions when developing an exposure plan.

Red or Black Card Game (page 32)

Ages: 8–12

Objective: Identify sources of anxiety, anxious thoughts, physiological symptoms of anxiety, and coping skills

Supplies: Standard 52-card deck; bag filled with small prizes

Advance Preparation:

Order the deck so there is an appropriate mix of red, black, and royalty cards.

Description:

This card game lowers the threat level of the assessment process. Positive feelings are explored first to ease the client into the activity. Points and prizes encourage openness and add to the appeal of the activity. Modify the worksheet if there are more pressing areas to assess.

People in My World (page 33)

Ages: 6–12

Objective: Assess family and community relationships

Supplies: Happy face stickers, star stickers, red marker, black marker

Description:

People in My World explores family and community relationships and available support networks. It also evaluates feelings such as happiness, sadness, and anger. Comfortable and uncomfortable feelings are both included in order to provide balance. The child should include self and significant family and community members on the worksheet (both positive and negative relationships) so that these relationships can be assessed. The practitioner completes the worksheet as the child places the stickers/symbols on the world. The activity is more appealing to children when happy face and star stickers are used; however, the child can draw if these stickers are not available. If the child has difficulty sitting and focusing, the outline of the world can be taped to the wall and the child can stand while placing the stickers/symbols on the world. As some children may censor their responses to protect their parents, it is best to complete this activity without the parents present.

Date: _____

Welcome_____ ,
   (Name of child)

This is a place where kids come to get help with their feelings and learn ways to feel better. You may be scared or nervous about being here today, but hopefully you'll feel better once we get to know each other. Each time you come here, I'll choose something for us to do first, then you get to choose what to do.

My job is to listen to you and to help you with your problems and worries. My job is also to help keep you safe, so if I'm ever worried about your safety, I will get help for you by talking to the adults whose job it is to protect children.

The games and activities we do together will help you talk about your feelings and learn ways to feel better. While I'll have lots of ideas about how I can help you, it's important that you have a say in what our plan will be when you come here, so we will talk about your ideas of what you would like help with.

All of the activities we do together will be put in this special book. I will keep your book for now. When you come here for the last time, you'll get to take your book home.

I look forward to talking and playing with you!

From,

_____

(Name of Therapist)

Jamie's Story
Chapter One: Getting Help

We're going to read a story. It's important that you listen carefully to the story so you can answer the questions. You get 1 point for each question you answer correctly. (Don't worry if you get the answer wrong. We'll read part of the story again, and then you will have the chance to answer again and earn a point.) At the end of the story, you can trade in points for prizes: 1–10 points = 1 prize; 11 or more points = 2 prizes.

Jamie's Story

This is a story about a kid named Jamie. Jamie loves to build forts, watch TV, and go bike riding. Jamie loves pizza, chocolate, and broccoli. Yup, that's right, Jamie loves broccoli!

Is this a story about a kid named Jamie?

Jamie loves to build forts, watch TV, and go bike riding. What is something you like to do?

Jamie loves pizza, chocolate, and broccoli. What is one of your favorite foods?

Jamie went to see a lady named Ana. Ana is a therapist. That means Ana's job is to help kids with their problems and worries. Ana said therapy is a place to get help for problems and worries, and learn ways to feel better.

Is Ana the name of Jamie's therapist?

What is the name of your therapist? (Hint: The person reading this story to you.)

Is a therapist's job to help kids with their problems and worries?

Is therapy a place to get help for problems and worries, and learn ways to feel better?

At first Jamie was nervous and shy with Ana. Jamie was so nervous and shy that Jamie clung to Mom and would not talk. Ana said, "Jamie, lots of kids are nervous and shy when they come here the first time. But you'll feel better once we get to know each other. Each time you come here, we will do some talking and some playing. We'll play some games and do other fun activities to help you talk about your feelings and learn ways to feel better. Don't worry: you won't have to talk about stuff until you are ready." Hearing this helped Jamie feel better. Jamie let go of Mom and went to sit beside Ana. Then Jamie and Ana played a fun game to get to know each other.

Are lots of kids nervous and shy when they meet a therapist?

Did Jamie feel better knowing that Ana would not make Jamie talk about stuff until Jamie was ready?

Did Jamie and Ana play a fun game to get to know each other?

You and your therapist are going to play a fun game to get to know each other. Ask your therapist to explain the game.

How About You?

Let's play a game to get to know each other better. It's called How About You? To play, we'll take turns throwing a ball back and forth and telling each other about our favorite things to do (see the example below). We'll play several rounds.

Player 1: I like to…(go to movies). How about you? (Player 1 throws the ball to Player 2.)

Player 2 catches the ball: I like to…(play computer games). How about you? (Player 2 throws the ball back to Player 1.)

Player 1 catches the ball: I like to…(bake cookies). How about you? (Player 1 throws the ball back to Player 2.)

Player 2 catches the ball: I like to…(ride my bike). How about you? (Player 2 throws the ball back to Player 1.)

And so on.

Five Favorites

Let's play the Five Favorites game to get to know each other better. To play, we'll take turns picking a game card from the bag and sharing with each other our favorite things. For example, if you pick from the bag the card that says "favorite animal," then we'll take turns saying our favorite animal. The game ends after we've picked all five cards from the bag and answered the five questions.

FAVORITE COLOR
FAVORITE FOOD
FAVORITE TV SHOW
FAVORITE ANIMAL
FAVORITE MOVIE

Sticky Dots

Everyone has problems and worries. This activity will help you talk about your problems and worries. Read each statement below and put a sticky dot beside the statements that apply to you. You can put more sticky dots to show how you feel (for example, if you don't feel this way at all, don't put any dots; if you feel this way a little put one or two dots; if you feel this way a lot put three or four dots; and if you feel this way all the time put five dots).

1. I WORRY ABOUT A LOT OF THINGS _____

2. I HAVE TROUBLE SLEEPING _____

3. I HAVE BAD DREAMS _____

4. I BELIEVE I CAN'T DO ANYTHING RIGHT _____

5. I DON'T LIKE THE WAY I LOOK _____

6. I OFTEN FEEL LONELY_____

7. I WORRY ABOUT GOING TO SCHOOL_____

8. I WORRY SOMETHING AWFUL WILL HAPPEN TO MY FAMILY_____

9. I HAVE SCARY MEMORIES OF BAD THINGS THAT HAPPENED TO ME _____

10. I OFTEN FEEL SICK _____

11. I LOSE MY TEMPER A LOT _____

12. I HURT MYSELF ON PURPOSE SOMETIMES _____

13. I GET INTO TROUBLE A LOT _____

14. I DON'T GET ALONG WELL WITH MY FAMILY_____

15. I THINK I'M IN THERAPY BECAUSE I'M BAD OR CRAZY_____

16. I GET TEASED BY OTHER KIDS_____

17. I FEEL SAD MUCH OF THE TIME_____

18. I HAVE AN UPSETTING SECRET THAT'S DIFFICULT TO TALK ABOUT_____

19. I WANT TO GET OVER MY FEARS BUT I'M NOT SURE HOW_____

Butterflies in My Stomach

Everyone has fears and worries. Some are small and some are big. This activity will help you talk about your fears and worries so we can eventually make a plan to help you handle them. It is called Butterflies in My Stomach because when you are scared or worried about something, your stomach might feel funny or jittery, as if you have butterflies in there! You don't really have butterflies in your stomach; it just feels like you do.

Write your fears and worries on the paper butterflies. Write each fear or worry on a separate paper butterfly. Write bigger fears or worries that bother you a lot on the larger butterflies, and write smaller fears or worries that don't bother you too much on the smaller ones. You can come up with your own fears and worries or you can choose from the list provided. (Some kids don't like to admit that they have a lot of fears and worries, but talking about them is an important step to getting help and to feeling better.)

Label the outside of a paper bag: FEARS AND WORRIES. After you write your worries on the paper butterflies, place them in the bag. Place some blank paper butterflies in the bag too, as you will add to the bag at a later time. The bag will be kept in the office so we can use it another time.

<u>List of Fears and Worries</u>

Being in the dark	Performing in a play or concert
Storms	Talking to people I don't know well
Getting kidnapped	Going to the doctor or dentist
War or terrorism	Getting an injection (needle)
Using a public toilet	Animals or insects
Getting sick or dying	Heights
Being away from parent	Vomiting
Sleeping in my own room	Blood
Going to school	Germs or dirt
Taking tests	Flying on an airplane
Making mistakes	Other fears or worries: _____

Butterfly Outlines

Red or Black Card Game

This game will help you talk about your thoughts and feelings. To play, pick up the top card from the deck of cards. If you get a red card, you get 1 point. If you get a black card, answer one of the questions below in order from 1 to 6. You get 2 points when you answer the question. If you pick a jack, queen, or king, you get 3 points! At the end of the game, trade in points for prizes: 1–10 points = 1 prize; 11 or more points = 2 prizes.

(1) What is something you enjoy doing?

(2) Say two things that make you feel happy.

(3) Say three things you worry about a lot.

(4) What kinds of things do you say to yourself when you're worried?

(5) Circle all the things that happen in your body when you feel worried:

STOMACH HURTS   HEAD ACHES   HOT/SWEATY

TIGHT MUSCLES   DIZZY   TROUBLE BREATHING

HEART BEATS FAST   OTHER: _____

(6) What helps you feel better when you are worried?

People in My World

This activity will help you talk about the important people in your world. Fill in the picture of the world by writing the names of the people in your world. Include people who are important because you feel close with them, as well as people who are important because they have hurt or upset you in some way. Write each person's name in a different section on the world. Be sure to include yourself, the people in your family, other people you live with, other adults who help take care of you, your teacher, and your therapist. You may wish to include other relatives or people you spend a lot of time with, such as grandparents, aunts, uncles, and close friends. Next, use stickers and symbols for the following feelings:

Put <u>happy faces</u> on anyone who feels <u>happy</u> most of the time. Why are they happy?

Draw <u>sad faces</u> on anyone who feels <u>sad</u> a lot. Why are they sad?

Put a <u>red X</u> on anyone who feels <u>angry</u> a lot. What makes them angry?

Put a <u>black X</u> on anyone who is <u>mean or bad</u>. Why are they mean or bad?

Put <u>stars</u> on anyone who <u>helps you</u> with your problems and worries. What do they do to help?

People in My World

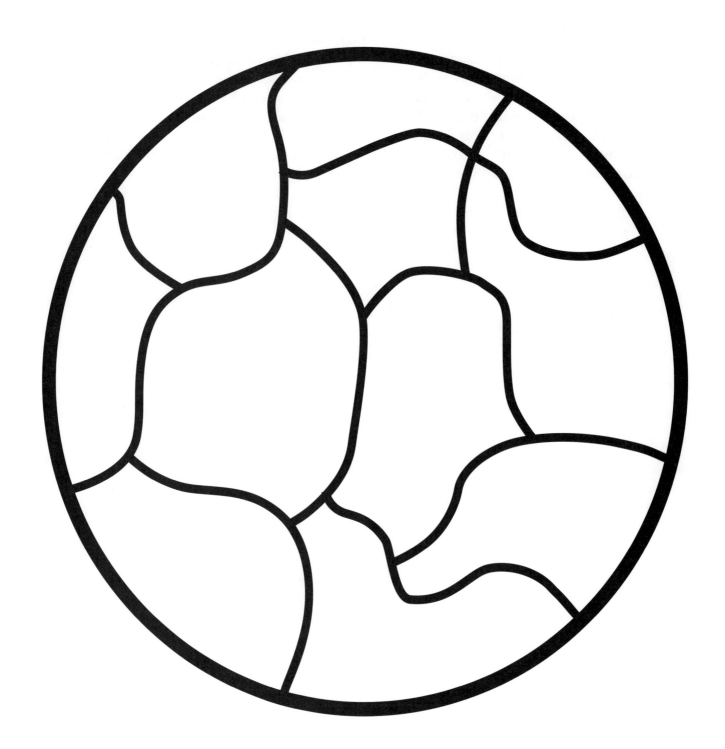

Section 3

Psychoeducation

Psychoeducation serves central key functions in cognitive behavioral therapy (CBT). The main purpose is to inform children and their parents about anxiety, sources of anxiety, symptoms of and common reactions to anxiety, and treatment approaches. This knowledge normalizes the client's experience of anxiety and empowers them to deal with anxiety in an optimal way.

When clients learn factual information about anxiety, misinformation is dispelled, and children and parents learn that others have faced similar challenges. As well, providing information on the effectiveness of CBT gives clients a sense of hope.

It is crucial to provide psychoeducation in an engaging manner so the client maintains interest and absorbs the material. Jamie's Story and the Crumpled Paper Throw game provide options for younger and older clients so practitioners can utilize the intervention that fits the client's developmental level.

Interventions

Jamie's Story (Chapter Two: Learning About Anxiety) (page 37)
Ages: 6–8
Objective: Explain anxiety, physiological responses to anxiety, benefits of therapy
Supplies: Bag filled with small prizes
Description:
The second chapter of Jamie's Story focuses on psychoeducation. The chapter defines and normalizes anxiety, describes physiological responses to anxiety, explains ways therapy can help, and instills a sense of hope.

Crumpled Paper Throw (page 39)
Ages: 8–12
Objective: Explain anxiety, physiological responses to anxiety, CBT, benefits of therapy
Supplies: Paper, masking tape, bag filled with small prizes
Description:
Crumpled Paper Throw helps children learn and process information on anxiety in a playful and developmentally appropriate manner. Review and modify the questions as needed to suit the needs of the client. Remove questions that are inappropriate to the child's situation. Prior to playing, place masking tape on the floor to create a "throw" line. The practitioner should stand at a distance from the line and form a hoop with their arms. It is important to stand far enough from the line to make the game challenging, but close enough to ensure

the client can have some success in throwing the crumpled paper through the hoop. Parents should play the game along with the child so they can learn together. Presumably, clients will not know the answers to many of the questions. However, they have the opportunity to learn the answers when the practitioner reads them aloud and can then earn points for providing the correct response. This approach encourages children to listen attentively when correct answers are read aloud, and facilitates learning and integration of the material. Children and parents can earn points that they can trade in at the end of the game for a small prize. Movement exercises are incorporated into the game to add to the appeal of the activity and to teach relaxation skills. The practitioner can participate in these movement exercises to model and to set a playful tone. The optional questions on specific anxiety disorders can be included, if appropriate. Providing specific information about a child's diagnosis can be helpful, as it normalizes the child's symptoms and behaviors.

Close Far Game (page 42)
Ages: 6–10
Objective: Identify body changes indicative of anxiety and stress
Supplies: Scissors, tape, blindfold (optional), bag filled with small prizes
Advance Preparation:
Cut out the body outline provided and tape it to a smooth wall or door at a height the client can reach. Cut out each Body Reaction and place a small piece of tape on the back of each one.

Description:
An important aspect of psychoeducation is teaching children the physiological responses to anxiety. The Close Far Game creates an awareness of body reactions to anxiety and normalizes these experiences. The game helps children learn in a safe environment and with the spirit of play. Since some children might feel anxious about being blindfolded, it is important to offer them the option of blindfolding their parent instead. Many children actually prefer this option, as they like the sense of control associated with it.

Jamie's Story
Chapter Two: Learning About Anxiety

Welcome back to the story!

Ana said, "Jamie, today we're going to learn about anxiety. 'Anxiety' is the word grown-ups use for feeling scared and worried a lot. Everyone feels scared and worried at times. A worry is when you think something bad is going to happen. For example, I worry that gigantic green elephants with purple polka dots will fall from the sky and smush my house...I'm just kidding. But there is something I'm actually worried about. I'm worried that it's going to rain tomorrow and I'll have to cancel the picnic I had planned. What do you worry about?" Jamie said, "I worry when I'm playing at the park that I'm gonna get chased by a dog. And I worry when Mom and Dad go out they won't come back. And I worry when it's my turn to read in front of the class that I'll do something stupid and everyone will laugh at me."

Is "anxiety" the word grown-ups use for feeling scared and worried a lot?

Is a worry when you think something bad is going to happen?

What is something Jamie worries about?

What is something you worry about?

Ana said, "Sometimes we feel a little worried and sometimes we feel a lot worried. Can you tell me a time you felt a little worried?" Jamie said, "When I spilled juice on my shirt, I worried my shirt was ruined. I was just a little worried because it wasn't my favorite shirt." Ana said, "That's a good example of a little worry. Can you tell me a time you felt a lot worried?" Jamie replied, "When it was the school play I felt a lot worried that I would forget my part and everyone would think I was stupid." Ana said, "That's a big worry that I'm sure lots of kids have."

Does Jamie sometimes feel a little worried and sometimes feel a lot worried?

Tell about a time you felt worried. Say if you felt a little or a lot worried.

Ana said, "When you are scared or worried your body feels different. You might get a sore tummy. Your body might get hot and sweaty. Your heart might beat really fast and you might have a hard time breathing. What sometimes happens in your body when you feel scared or worried?" Jamie said, "When I feel scared or worried my tummy hurts. And sometimes my heart beats faster."

When Jamie feels scared or worried does Jamie's tummy hurt and does Jamie's heart beat faster?

What is one thing that sometimes happens in your body when you feel scared or worried?

Ana said, "Sometimes when kids are worried, it stops them from having fun. Does that ever happen to you?" Jamie said, "Yup! Like when I'm at the park I don't have much fun because I'm worried about getting chased by a dog. And when I'm at my friend's house I don't have much fun because I'm scared to be away from Mom and Dad."

Do worries sometimes make it hard for kids to have fun?

Ana explained to Jamie, "Therapy will help you learn special skills to cope with fears and worries. One of the special skills you will learn in therapy is how to relax your body. Once you learn these special skills, worries won't get in the way of having fun. This will help you feel more relaxed and happier." Jamie wanted to have more fun. Jamie wanted to feel more relaxed and happier. So Jamie was excited to come back to therapy to learn special skills to cope with fears and worries.

Is learning to relax your body one of the special skills that can help you cope with worried feelings?

Is learning to hop on one foot while holding a giant green elephant with purple polka dots one of the special skills that can help you cope with worried feelings?

Crumpled Paper Throw

Crumpled Paper Throw will help you learn about anxiety. To play, crumple a piece of paper into a ball, stand behind the tape line, and throw the paper ball toward the hoop I will make with my arms. If you get the crumpled paper through the hoop, you earn 1 point. If you miss, I will ask you a question. (The questions are about anxiety.) You get 2 points for each question you answer correctly. If your answer is incorrect, I will read the answer to the question, and then you will have the chance to answer again and earn 2 points. (Don't worry if you get the answer wrong the first time—the whole point of the game is to learn about anxiety, so that's why I'll read the answer and then give you a second chance to say what you think the answer is.) At the end of the game, trade in points for prizes: 1–10 points = 1 prize; 11 or more points = 2 prizes.

Question: What is therapy?
Answer: Therapy is a place where people get help for their problems and worries.

Question: What is a therapist?
Answer: A therapist is a person to talk to about problems and worries. It may take some time to feel comfortable talking to a therapist about problems and worries.

Question: What is anxiety?
Answer: Anxiety is a feeling of worry or nervousness. Everyone gets anxious or worried sometimes. When kids worry a lot, it can be hard for them to feel happy and enjoy certain activities. Kids need help for anxiety when they worry much of the time, and when their fears or worries stop them from having fun or from doing normal activities.

Take a break to move your body: Do the shoulder scrunch by scrunching your shoulders up to your ears, then relaxing them and moving them around five times.

Question: True or Not True: Many kids feel scared or embarrassed to admit that they feel afraid, anxious, or worried a lot.
Answer: True. Many kids find it hard to admit that they're scared and worried. Some kids may think they should act tougher or that they're too old to be scared. It's important for kids to know that it's okay to have worries and fears. Admitting that you have a lot of worries and fears is the first step to getting help and to feeling better!

Question: What are some common things that kids with anxiety worry about?
Answer: Kids with anxiety often worry that bad things will happen to them or to their family. They might feel afraid to be away from their parent(s). They might feel afraid of things like bugs, dogs, or the dark. They might be afraid going to parties or being around people they don't know.

Question: What does anxiety feel like in the body?
Answer: When you feel anxious or worried, you might get a sore tummy or have diarrhea. Your body might get hot and sweaty. You might feel dizzy or shaky, or even feel like you're going to throw up or faint. Your heart might pound really fast and you might

have a hard time breathing. Therapy can help you learn ways to handle anxiety so your body doesn't feel so bad.

Take a break to move your body: Stretch your body by lacing your fingers together and raising your hands above your head, palms facing upward. Hold this pose for five seconds.

Question: What is the fight, flight, freeze response?
Answer: When a person thinks that something dangerous is about to happen, their body makes chemicals that get them to fight off the danger OR run away from the danger (flight) OR get very still (freeze). The fight, flight, freeze response can protect you when there is real danger, but it can be a problem when there is no real danger. For example, let's say you are afraid of dogs. You are at the park and you see a dog. The dog is not doing anything dangerous. But because you are afraid of dogs, you think this dog is dangerous. You might react in one of three ways: (1) You hit the dog with a stick (fight); (2) You run away from the dog (flight); 3) You are unable to move (freeze). Therapy can help you learn ways to tell your brain and body to react differently so you can cope better with scary situations.

Question: True or Not True: Some anxiety can be helpful.
Answer: True. Anxiety can actually be helpful because it can protect people from real danger. For example, if you're crossing the street and a car comes fast toward you, anxiety would alert you to this danger so you can get out of the car's way.

Take a break to move your body: Do neck circles by placing your hands on your hips, and circling your head in one direction three times, then in the opposite direction three times.

Question: What is cognitive behavioral therapy (CBT)?
Answer: Cognitive behavioral therapy, or CBT for short, is a type of therapy to help people with anxiety. In CBT, kids learn special skills to help them cope with worries and fears. CBT has proven to be the best way to help kids deal with anxiety.

Question: What is gradual exposure?
Answer: Gradual exposure is part of CBT. Gradual exposure involves facing a fear a little at a time until the fear is not so scary anymore. Don't worry: We will only start this part of therapy when you are ready. We will make a plan together so you feel okay with it. After a while, your anxiety will lessen and you will feel calmer and better.

Question: True or Not True: The goal of therapy is to make anxiety go away.
Answer: Not True. Remember, some anxiety is normal and helpful, so we need a certain amount of anxiety. The goal of therapy is to help kids handle fears and worries so anxiety does not stop them from having fun or from doing normal activities.

Take a break to move your body: You did a great job learning about anxiety. Give yourself a pat on the back!

Optional Questions
(Only include if appropriate for the client)

Question: What is separation anxiety?
Answer: Separation anxiety is when children feel really scared to be away from their parent(s). They may get scared when their parents leave them with a babysitter or when they're dropped off at a friend's home. Therapy will help you learn ways to handle being away from your parent(s) so you don't miss out on fun, and so you can feel calmer and happier.

Question: What is social anxiety?
Answer: Kids who have social anxiety feel really scared when they are around people they don't know well. This makes it hard for them to meet new people, go to parties or camp, or join a team. Therapy will help you learn ways to feel safe around people you don't know well.

Question: What is selective mutism?
Answer: Selective mutism is when a child does not speak in some situations but speaks comfortably in other situations. Kids with selective mutism might not speak at school or around people they don't know well, but they're usually comfortable speaking at home.

Question: What is a phobia?
Answer: A phobia is an extreme fear to a thing or a situation. The thing or situation is not actually as dangerous as the person thinks it is. But to the person with the phobia, the danger feels real because the fear feels so huge. Phobias cause people to worry about and avoid the things or situations they fear. Having a phobia can stop you from enjoying normal activities. Therapy will help you learn ways to deal with your phobia.

Question: What is obsessive-compulsive disorder (OCD)?
Answer: OCD causes someone to have worrying thoughts (obsessions) or repeated behaviors (compulsions) that they don't want but cannot stop, no matter how hard they try. Therapy will help you learn ways to get control over OCD.

Question: What is a panic attack?
Answer: A panic attack is when the anxiety gets so strong that it seems to take over your whole body. For example, you can have a hard time breathing. You might also notice that your heart beats faster and you feel dizzy or sweaty. Therapy can help you learn to handle or prevent panic attacks.

Close Far Game

When you are scared or worried, your body feels different. You might get a sore stomach or have diarrhea. Your body might get hot and sweaty. You might feel dizzy or even feel like you're going to throw up or faint. Your heart might beat really fast and you might have a hard time breathing. It's important to talk about what happens in your body when you are anxious or worried so you can learn ways to help your body feel better.

The Close Far game will help you talk about what happens in your body when you feel scared or worried. To play, stand about three feet away from the wall where the Body Outline is hanging and face the wall. Your parent will put a blindfold on you and place in your hand a piece of paper. The paper will contain words that describe a body reaction—something you might feel when you are anxious of worried. The paper has a piece of tape attached to it. Walk toward the Body Outline and try to stick the Body Reaction onto it. Your parent will say "close" or "far" to help you stick the Body Reaction onto the body outline. You get 2 points for each Body Reaction that you stick onto the body outline. Continue the game until you have used all of the Body Reactions. (If you prefer, your parent can be the one wearing the blindfold, and you can say "close" or "far" to help your parent get the Body Reaction onto the body outline. Your parent can earn points for you!) At the end of the game, trade in points for prizes:
1-10 points = 1 prize; 11 or more points = 2 prizes.

After the game, talk about the ways your body reacts when you feel scared or worried.

Body Reactions

FAST HEARTBEAT	TIGHT MUSCLES	SORE TUMMY
DIARRHEA	HOT AND SWEATY	DIZZY
FIDGETY FEET	DRY MOUTH	TROUBLE BREATHING

Close Far Game
Body Reactions Outline

Information Sheet for Parents:
Learning About Anxiety

Key Points

- Some anxiety is normal, helpful, and necessary. Anxiety can protect people from real danger. Kids need help for anxiety when they worry much of the time, and when their fears or worries stop them from enjoying normal activities.

- Cognitive behavioral therapy, or CBT, is a type of therapy to help people with anxiety. In CBT, kids learn coping skills, like relaxation techniques, and they learn to face their fears.

- Gradual exposure is part of CBT. Gradual exposure involves facing a fear a little at a time until the fear is not so scary anymore. Gradual exposure will be introduced in therapy when your child is ready. We will develop a step-by-step plan together so you and your child feel okay with it. We will talk more about gradual exposure when we are ready to start that part of therapy.

Tips

Since children learn best when important information is repeated several times, you can help your child by reinforcing what was learned in today's session. Below are some helpful messages you can say to your child when the time seems appropriate:

- Many kids find it hard to admit that they're scared and worried. Talking to me and to your therapist about your worries and fears is an important step to feeling better!

- You are not in therapy because you are weird, crazy, or bad. Lots of people see a therapist to help them deal with problems and worries.

- You have a stomachache (or other physical symptom) because you are feeling scared or worried. In therapy, you will learn ways to handle fears and worries so your body doesn't feel so bad.

Educating yourself about anxiety will help you better support your child. The Internet is a great source of free resources and articles. There are also many books on the topic. See the next page for recommended resources.

Resources for Parents on Childhood Anxiety

Websites

Anxiety and Depression Association of America: www.adaa.org

AnxietyBC: www.anxietybc.com

Anxiety Wellness Center: www.anxietywellness.com

Worry Wise Kids: www.worrywisekids.org

Resources

Worried No More: Help and Hope for Anxious Children by A. Wagner (2005)

Worried No More: The One-Hour Workshop for Parents (CD Rom) by A. Wagner (Available at www.anxietywellness.com)

Anxious Kids, Anxious Parents: 7 Ways to Stop the Worry Cycle and Raise Courageous and Independent Children by R. Wilson and L. Lyons (2013)

The Worried Child: Recognizing Anxiety in Children and Helping Them Heal by P. Foxman (2004)

The Opposite of Worry: The Playful Parenting Approach to Childhood Anxieties and Fears by L. Cohen (2013)

Section 4

Relaxation

Relaxation training helps anxious children develop awareness and control over their own physiological and muscular responses to anxiety. Two of the most commonly used and effective relaxation skills are deep breathing and progressive muscle relaxation (PMR). Deep breathing (also known as diaphragmatic breathing) involves slow, deep breaths through the diaphragm to initiate the body's relaxation response. Diaphragmatic breathing is an important skill to master because people who are anxious often hyperventilate, taking quick shallow breaths that can trigger rapid heartbeat, lightheadedness, and other symptoms. PMR involves purposefully tensing and then relaxing muscles in the body.

Children who are highly anxious are often resistant to relaxation. This may be due to a pessimistic mental assessment (e.g.,"This won't work") or extreme feelings of fear that prevent them from relaxing (Cohen, 2013). Teaching children to relax by making it into a fun game is often an effective way to break through the resistive barrier. For some children, the task of focusing on bodily sensations is itself anxiety provoking. Highly anxious children may "scan their bodies for any signal of distress and catastrophically misinterpret normal bodily reactions" (Friedberg & McClure, 2015, p. 282). Children may also fear losing control. Children's anxiety can be addressed by setting up the relaxation exercise as an experiment (e.g., "What do you think might happen?") (Friedberg & McClure, 2015, p. 282).

Children are more open to using a relaxation strategy when they feel they are in charge. Thus, several relaxation techniques are outlined in this chapter so children can learn more than one strategy and can choose the one they like best. Once the client has learned the relaxation strategy, it is helpful to begin each subsequent session with a few rounds. This will facilitate further mastery and set a relaxed tone for the session.

The homework exercises included in this section encourage practicing and facilitate integration of skills. Parents are encouraged to incorporate the relaxation strategy into a calm and nurturing daily bedtime routine for the child. It is important to emphasize to clients that relaxation skills must be learned before they can be used appropriately to manage anxiety.

Interventions

Cookie Breathing Game (page 49)
Ages: 6–10
Objective: Apply diaphragmatic breathing to decrease anxiety
Supplies: Dice, scissors, bag, markers, bag filled with small prizes
Advance Preparation:
Cut out the six cookies and place them in a bag.
Description:
Making diaphragmatic breathing fun and easy to learn will motivate children to use this relaxation strategy. When first learning Cookie Breathing, clients often continue to take deep breaths through their chest rather than through their diaphragm. The practitioner can demonstrate this error by doing Cookie Breathing the wrong way (taking deep breaths through the chest) then doing it the correct way (taking deep breaths through the diaphragm). As the practitioner demonstrates deep breathing, the child can guess which is the correct method. Parents should be included in the session, as they also benefit from learning diaphragmatic breathing. As well, parents need to learn the technique so they can coach the child to practice and can cue the child to use diaphragmatic breathing when the child needs to de-stress.

Awesome App (page 53)
Ages: 10–16
Objective: Apply diaphragmatic breathing to decrease anxiety
Supplies: Smartphone or tablet with Internet connection
Description:
Using smartphone or tablet applications, or apps, in therapy is an *effective* way to motivate older children to learn and practice relaxation skills. Deep breathing apps *must* be screened prior to the session to ensure they are appropriate for the client, easy to use, and effectively teach diaphragmatic deep breathing. If the client responds well to the use of apps to learn relaxation, the intervention can be repeated using other apps to learn mindfulness, guided meditation, and journaling.

Tight-Relax Game (page 55)
Ages: 6–8
Objective: Utilize muscle relaxation to decrease anxiety
Supplies: Dice, bag filled with small prizes
Description:
This activity teaches muscle relaxation, which is a helpful technique to relieve anxiety. The game format and rewards motivate children to learn. The Tight-Relax technique involves tightening then relaxing the whole body at once, rather than progressively relaxing each muscle group, because children typically lack the patience involved in progressive muscle relaxation. The parents should learn the technique so they can coach the child to practice and can cue the child to use a relaxation strategy when the child needs to de-stress. (Note: The Tight-Relax technique is not an original concept, as many authors have published similar interventions involving PMR.)

Cookie Breathing Game

When you are anxious or worried, your body feels tight and uncomfortable. Learning how to take deep breaths is a good way to calm your body so you can feel better. Cookie Breathing is a special way of breathing that can help your body relax and control scared, anxious feelings. Follow the steps below:

Step 1: Put your hand on your tummy, where your belly button is. Slowly breathe in and out. When you breathe in, your tummy should move out. When you breathe out, your tummy should move in. Breathe in and out like this four times and feel your tummy move in and out. When doing Cookie Breathing, make sure your shoulders and chest are relaxed and still. Only your tummy should be moving in and out.

Step 2: Continue this special way of breathing, but now when you breathe in, do it through your nose for three seconds, and when you breathe out, do it through your mouth for four seconds. To help you do this, imagine a yummy batch of cookies that just came out of the oven. As you breathe in, smell those yummy cookies! But they're hot, so you have to blow on them to cool them down. As you breathe out, blow on the cookies to cool them down.

Remember:
Smell the cookies: Breathe in through your nose for three seconds, tummy moves out.
Blow on the cookies: Breathe out through your mouth for four seconds, tummy moves in.

(When first learning Cookie Breathing, it helps to do it lying down. You can put a small toy or book on your tummy and watch it go up and down as you breathe.)

Let's do an experiment to see how your body feels when it is stressed or anxious, and how you can use Cookie Breathing to calm your body. Follow the steps below:

Step 1: Notice how your body feels when it is calm. Circle 1 or 2 below to show what you notice about your body:

(1) Heart is beating at a normal rate; body temperature is normal; I'm breathing normally.
         or
(2) Heart is beating very fast; I'm hot and sweaty; it's hard to breathe.

Step 2: Do jumping jacks until you are <u>very</u> out of breath (at least 40 to 60 seconds). Don't worry: this is not dangerous! Notice how your body feels when it is <u>stressed</u>. Circle 1 or 2 below to show what you notice about your body:

(1) Heart is beating at a normal rate; body temperature is normal; I'm breathing normally.

       or

(2) Heart is beating fast; I'm hot and sweaty; it's hard to breathe.

Step 3: Do jumping jacks again until you are <u>very</u> out of breath (at least 40 to 60 seconds). Then use Cookie Breathing to relax your body. Do Cookie Breathing until your body is back to a calm state (e.g., your heart is beating at a normal rate and you are breathing normally).

Put a checkmark beside the statements below that show what you learned from this experiment:

___ My body changes when I am stressed or anxious.
___ Doing Cookie Breathing relaxes my body.

Put a checkmark beside the answer you think is best:

___ If I am starting to feel stressed or anxious, I should wait to do Cookie Breathing until my heart is beating very fast and I am having trouble breathing.

___ I should do Cookie Breathing as soon as I start to feel stressed or anxious. This will help me keep calm.

Do Cookie Breathing again, but this time, think about your favorite kind of cookie, hot out of the oven. Imagine you are smelling the cookies and blowing on them to cool them down.

When you are feeling scared or worried and you do Cookie Breathing at the same time as you are thinking of your favorite kind of cookie, you relax your body. You also replace your scared, worried thoughts with happy thoughts about your favorite kind of cookie!

Let's play the Cookie Breathing game to help you practice. To play, roll the dice. If you roll an even number, do Cookie Breathing properly and slowly two times. If you roll an odd number, pick two paper cookies from the bag. Play until you have collected all six paper cookies. You get a prize once you have collected all six paper cookies.

Cookie Breathing Game: Cookies

Practice Activity to Do at Home:
Cookie Breathing

Do Cookie Breathing properly ten times each night before bedtime. It will help your body relax in preparation for sleep. It's best to do Cookie Breathing together with your parent. If you practice Cookie Breathing every night, you will get good at it so you can use it when you need to relax your body.

Instructions for Cookie Breathing

Think of my favorite cookies hot out of the oven. Smell the yummy cookies: <u>Breathe in through my nose for three seconds</u>, tummy moves out.

Think of my favorite cookies hot out of the oven. Blow on the cookies to cool them down: <u>Breathe out through my mouth for four seconds</u>, tummy moves in.

Use the chart below to help you keep track. Put a checkmark in the box each time you do Cookie Breathing.

MONDAY	TUESDAY	WEDNESDAY	THURSDAY	FRIDAY	SATURDAY	SUNDAY

Awesome App

When you feel anxious or worried, your breathing might speed up. This can feel uncomfortable and make you feel even more anxious. Deep breathing exercises are an easy and effective way to reduce stress and anxiety. Although deep breathing may seem like an easy thing to do, many people actually do it wrong—they take deep breaths using their chest and shoulders rather than their diaphragm. Taking deep breaths using your chest and shoulders isn't relaxing at all! Proper breathing can be hard to learn. Fortunately, there's an app for almost anything, including deep breathing. Since there are many deep breathing apps to choose from, it's important to find the one that's right for you. Explore two or three deep breathing apps (make sure the apps teach diaphragmatic breathing), note what you like/don't like about each app (see below), then choose your favorite.

Name of app: _____

Features I like: _____

Features I don't like: _____

Name of app: _____

Features I like: _____

Features I don't like: _____

Name of app: _____

Features I like: _____

Features I don't like: _____

Once you have chosen your favorite app and used it to learn diaphragmatic deep breathing, it's time to practice. Have your deep breathing app ready to go. Run in place for one minute. Notice how your breathing speeds up. (Your breathing also speeds up when you are anxious, so it's good to be aware of these physical feelings.) Then use your app to guide you through diaphragmatic deep breathing. Do diaphragmatic deep breathing until your breathing slows completely back to normal. Notice how you are able to relax your body.

Diaphragmatic deep breathing is a technique you can use anywhere, anytime. It can help lower anxiety and give you a sense of control. Diaphragmatic deep breathing can also give you more energy and leads to better concentration. But in order to use it effectively, you have to become good at it. Practice each night before bedtime. This is the best time to practice because it will relax your body in preparation for sleep. You can use the deep breathing app or do it on your own. It's a good idea to do ten rounds of diaphragmatic deep breathing each night so your body really becomes relaxed. Use the chart on the next page to help you keep track.

Practice Activity to Do at Home:
Diaphragmatic Deep Breathing

Do diaphragmatic deep breathing properly each night before bedtime. You can use the deep breathing app or do it on your own. It's a good idea to do ten rounds of diaphragmatic deep breathing each night so your body really becomes relaxed. Use the chart below to help you keep track. Put a checkmark in the box each time you do diaphragmatic deep breathing.

MONDAY	TUESDAY	WEDNESDAY	THURSDAY	FRIDAY	SATURDAY	SUNDAY

Tight-Relax Game

When you feel anxious, the muscles in your body get tight and tense. This can feel uncomfortable and make you feel even more scared or worried. Learning how to relax your muscles is a good way to feel calm again. The Tight-Relax game will help you learn to relax your muscles. Since it is impossible to feel anxious and relaxed at the same time, this is a great way for you to control scared, worried feelings. Follow the steps below:

Step 1: Stand up straight and stiff like a stick, clench your fists, and tighten all the parts of your body from your head to your toes. Hold this tight pose for three seconds.
Tip: Make your muscles go tight but not so tight that they hurt.

Step 2: Unclench your fists and make your body go floppy like a wet noodle. Feel how all your muscles are relaxed. Hold this relaxed pose for three seconds.

Now let's play the Tight-Relax game to help you practice. To play, roll the dice. The number that you roll will let you know how many times to do the tight-relax pose. For example, if you roll a 2, then do the tight-relax pose two times. If you roll a 5, then do the tight-relax pose five times. If you roll the same number again, keep rolling until you get a number you have not yet rolled (and only do the Tight-Relax pose when you role a new number).

Play until you have rolled each number on the dice. You get a prize once you have rolled all six numbers. To help you keep track, check off each time you roll a different number.

1 _____
2 _____
3 _____
4 _____
5 _____
6 _____

Practice Activity to Do at Home:
Tight-Relax Pose

Do the tight-relax pose five times each night before bedtime. It will help your body relax in preparation for sleep. If you practice this every night, you will get good at it so you can use it when you need to help your body relax. It's best to do the tight-relax pose together with your parent.

Instructions for the Tight-Relax Pose

Step 1: Stand up straight and stiff like a stick, clench my fists and tighten all the parts of my body from my head to my toes. Hold this tight pose for three seconds.

Step 2: Unclench my fists and make my body go floppy like a wet noodle. Hold this relaxed pose for three seconds.

Use the chart below to keep track. Put a checkmark in the box each time you do the tight-relax pose.

MONDAY	TUESDAY	WEDNESDAY	THURSDAY	FRIDAY	SATURDAY	SUNDAY

Information Sheet for Parents: Relaxation

Key Points

- Learning relaxation skills is an important part of managing anxiety. When children are relaxed, they are calmer, able to concentrate better, and have a more restful sleep.

- Two of the most commonly used and effective relaxation skills are deep breathing (also known as diaphragmatic breathing) and progressive muscle relaxation (PMR). Deep breathing involves slow, deep breaths through the diaphragm to initiate the body's relaxation response. (The diaphragm is the area on the stomach just above the belly button.) PMR involves purposefully tensing and then relaxing muscles in the body.

- Fun, easy-to-use techniques will motivate your child to learn relaxation skills.

- Relaxation skills require repeated practice before they can be effectively used to manage anxiety.

Tips

- If your child practices daily, they will learn the relaxation technique so it can be used to cope with fear and anxiety.
- Establish a bedtime routine that includes relaxation. A routine means you do the same things in the same order and at the same time every day. For example: at 7:30 p.m., your child takes a warm bath, then puts on pajamas and brushes teeth. By 8 p.m., your child is in bed and you read a bedtime story while cuddling together until 8:15 p.m. Then you do the relaxation technique five times, give hugs and kisses goodnight, and turn the lights out by 8:30 p.m. A new routine might take a few weeks to establish, but this process will go more smoothly if you stick to the same schedule and procedure each night.
- Do the relaxation technique along with your child—it will help your child learn the technique and it will reduce your stress level too!
- Once the relaxation technique has been learned, you can encourage its use when de-stressing is needed. You can follow this four-step process:

1. Pay attention to the signs that your child is getting overly scared or anxious, and name what you see: "You're holding on to me very tightly and you have a scared look on your face."

57

2. Coach your child to use the relaxation technique to get calm (do the relaxation technique too so your child can follow your lead). For example, say, "Let's do (Cookie Breathing/Tight-Relax Pose) together to get calm. We'll do it a few times until our bodies feel calm."

3. Praise your child: "You just did a great job doing (Cookie Breathing/Tight-Relax Pose) to calm your body."

4. Empower your child: "You have the power to make your body get calm."

   • If your child is in a highly anxious state, help bring the anxiety down to a more manageable level. For example, you can gently rub their back or give them space. Once your child is in a more receptive state, you can then apply the four steps above.

   • Model the relaxation technique by using it at appropriate times. For example, while stuck in traffic, take some slow deep breaths and say to your child, "I'm so frustrated that we're stuck in traffic, but doing Cookie Breathing five times really helped me to get calm and feel better."

   • It might be helpful for your child's teacher to learn the relaxation technique so your child can be prompted to utilize the strategy to de-stress at school. To avoid any unnecessary embarrassment, your child and teacher can come up with a secret signal that will serve as a visual reminder for your child to use the relaxation strategy.

Section 5

Affective Expression

Many children have difficulty naming feelings and being able to differentiate between emotions. A central goal in cognitive behavioral therapy (CBT) is to help children develop awareness of internal emotional states and to be able to appropriately label what they are feeling.

Some children benefit from more than one session on this component. Techniques from other sources can be integrated into therapy sessions. Feelings Tic-Tac-Toe (Lowenstein, 1999), Feelings Ring Toss (Dyson, 2011), Fruit Loop Feelings Necklace (Goodyear-Brown, 2002), and Lego Emotion House (Grant, 2014) are fun activities that encourage the expression of emotions. Letting the Cat Out of the Bag (Lowenstein, 2002) helps children match feelings with facial expressions and body poses. Mancala Feeling Stones (Van Hollander, 2011) allows children to quantify feelings. In addition to the many techniques from which to choose, there are toys that can help children identify and express feelings, such as Meebie and Kimochis Cloud. A feelings poster is another helpful tool (available at specialty retailers). Utilizing a variety of playful interventions and tools helps children strengthen affective expression and modulation skills.

Parents play an important role in helping their child openly express feelings. Including parents (and possibly the whole family) in sessions can facilitate open communication.

Interventions

Jamie's Story (Chapter Three: Feelings) (page 61)
Ages: 5–8
Objective: Verbally articulate a range of feelings and their intensity
Supplies: Bag filled with small prizes
Description:
Jamie's Story defines a variety of emotional states and helps children label their feelings. Examples are provided for each emotion to which children can generally relate. Clients then share their own examples for the various feelings. The concept of feeling intensity is taught and integrated into the story. Scaling the intensity of feelings is an important concept for children to master at this stage of therapy so they can apply it to exposure tasks in later stages of treatment.

Guess Which Hand (page 63)
Ages: 6–10
Objective: Verbally articulate a range of feelings and their intensity
Supplies: Scissors, bag filled with small prizes
Advance Preparation:
Cut out each Feeling-Word Square.

Description:

This game helps children expand their emotional vocabulary, label feelings, and rate their intensity. Definitions are provided for each feeling. However, some children will require added explanations using examples that they understand and can relate to. For example, "Brave is when you do something that's scary, like jumping into the deep end of the swimming pool for the first time." Once children comprehend each of the Feeling Words, they are better able to ascribe feelings to situations in their own lives. As the child talks about feelings, the practitioner can make reflective comments, ask the child to elaborate, and praise the child for openness. The Feeling Words for the game have been specifically ordered so that primary emotions (happy, sad, angry, scared) are chosen first. The concept of feeling intensity is taught and integrated into the game. Scaling the intensity of feelings is an important concept for children to master at this stage of therapy so they can apply it to exposure tasks in later stages of treatment. Some children will get upset when they do not guess the correct hand—use this as a teachable moment to help the client control upset through positive self-talk. Children have limited attention spans and can only manage a few rounds of the game. Use clinical discretion to determine how many rounds to play and which emotions to select. A few quick rounds can be played at the beginning of subsequent sessions to continue to build the child's emotional vocabulary. During the game, write the child's responses for each feeling on the appropriate feeling square.

Air Hockey Feelings Game (page 65)

Ages: 8–12

Objective: Verbally articulate a range of feelings and their intensity

Supplies: Two straws, masking tape, marker, scissors, timer, bag filled with small prizes

Advance Preparation:

Make the air hockey rink (see the instructions provided on page 66). Cut out the Feeling-Word Squares, and place them face up on the table.

Description:

Air Hockey Feelings is an intervention that lowers defenses and creates a playful format from which various feeling states can be identified and processed. Definitions are provided for each feeling. However, the practitioner can offer additional explanations using examples that children understand and can relate to. As the child talks about feelings, the practitioner can make reflective comments, ask the child to elaborate, and praise the child for openness. When it is the practitioner's turn to share, responses can be tailored in a way that would be therapeutically beneficial to the child. The Feeling Words for the game have been specifically ordered so that primary emotions (happy, sad, angry, scared) are chosen first. The concept of feeling intensity is taught and integrated into the game. Scaling the intensity of feelings is an important concept for children to master at this stage of therapy so they can apply it to exposure tasks in later stages of treatment. Children have limited attention spans and can only manage a few rounds of the game. Use clinical discretion to determine how many rounds to play. The practitioner participates along with the child and should be animated and energetic to maintain a playful tone. The client and practitioner work collaboratively to blow the puck from one end of the rink to the other—this strengthens the therapeutic rapport. Timing each round and working together to try to beat the record adds another element of playfulness to the activity.

Jamie's Story
Chapter Three: Feelings

Welcome back to the story!

When Jamie came to see Ana, Jamie looked happy. Ana said, "Jamie, you look really happy today. How come you're so happy?" Jamie replied, "I went to the dentist." Ana was surprised. Ana said, "I'm surprised to hear that going to the dentist made you happy." Jamie said, "Well, I wasn't happy at first but now I am." Ana asked Jamie to tell her all about going to the dentist. Jamie said, "I'll tell you about the NOT happy part first. When Mom told me I was going to the dentist I was very <u>worried</u> because I thought it was going to hurt. And I was <u>angry</u> at Mom for making me go."

<u>Worried</u> is feeling afraid something bad is going to happen. At first, Jamie was very <u>worried</u> about going to the dentist because Jamie thought it was going to hurt. Tell about a time you felt <u>worried</u>.

<u>Angry</u> is how you feel when you don't like what's happening. Jamie was <u>angry</u> at Mom for making Jamie go to the dentist. Tell about a time you felt <u>angry</u>.

"When I got to the dentist I sat in the big special chair. The dentist could see I didn't want to be there so the dentist let me press the button to make the big chair go way down. That was pretty fun! Then the dentist said it was time to take an X-ray of my mouth. The dentist explained that an X-ray is a special kind of picture. The X-ray would help the dentist check my teeth properly. Then the dentist put a heavy cover on me. This made me feel <u>scared</u> so I started to cry and scream. I even kicked the dentist! This made Mom cross. Mom said kicking the dentist is not okay behavior. Mom said to do Cookie Breathing to get calm. So I did Cookie Breathing and it calmed me down! Mom and the dentist were <u>proud</u> of me for doing Cookie Breathing to get calm. I felt <u>proud</u> of me too! But I also felt <u>guilty</u> for kicking the dentist because I knew that was a bad thing to do. I said sorry to the dentist. The dentist explained that the heavy cover and the X-ray are not dangerous and won't hurt. The cover will just feel a little weird. Knowing the heavy cover and X-ray would not be dangerous and would not hurt made me feel better."

<u>Scared</u> is feeling afraid that something dangerous is happening. Jamie felt <u>scared</u> of the heavy cover for the X-ray. Tell about a time you felt <u>scared</u>.

<u>Proud</u> is feeling good about something you did well. Jamie felt <u>proud</u> for doing Cookie Breathing to get calm. Tell about a time you felt <u>proud</u>.

<u>Guilty</u> is feeling bad for doing something wrong. Jamie felt <u>guilty</u> for kicking the dentist. Tell about a time you felt <u>guilty</u>.

"After I got the X-ray the dentist checked my teeth. The dentist poked my teeth with a sharp thing. This made me feel scared but I decided to be <u>brave</u> and let the dentist do it without making another fuss. The dentist could see that I looked scared and said, 'Jamie, don't be scared. This is just a tool I use to check your teeth. It won't hurt.' Hearing this helped me feel better. Plus the dentist was right—it didn't hurt!"

<u>Brave</u> means doing something scary. Jamie felt <u>brave</u> for letting the dentist poke Jamie's teeth with the sharp thing. Tell about a time you felt <u>brave</u>.

"Then the dentist said I was all done and I could get a toy from the special toy box. I looked through the toy box but I could not find a sparkly bouncy ball like the one my sister got. This made me feel <u>jealous</u> of my sister. But then the dentist checked for one in the back room. And guess what? The dentist found a sparkly bouncy ball—the kind I wanted! This made me feel <u>happy</u>!"

<u>Jealous</u> is how you feel when someone has something you want. Jamie felt jealous because Jamie wanted a sparkly bouncy ball like the one Jamie's sister got. Tell about a time you felt <u>jealous</u>.

<u>Happy</u> is how you feel when something good happens. Jamie felt happy because the dentist found a sparkly ball, the kind Jamie wanted. Tell about a time you felt <u>happy</u>.

Ana said, "Jamie, it sounds like you experienced many different feelings at the dentist. I'm proud of you for doing such a good job talking to me today about your feelings. Talking about feelings is a good way to cope and feel better."

Is Ana proud of Jamie for doing such a good job talking about feelings?

Is talking about feelings a good way to cope and feel better?

Guess Which Hand

We all experience different feelings. Feelings are what we feel inside about people or situations, like happy, sad, angry, or scared. The Guess Which Hand game will help you talk about feelings. I will pick up a Feeling-Word Square (e.g., happy), fold it several times to form a small paper clump, and place it in one hand. I will then put my hands behind my back and move the folded square from hand to hand a few times. Then, I will place both of my hands in front of me and ask you to guess which hand is holding the folded Feeling-Word Square. If you guess the correct hand, tell about a time you experienced the feeling. You get 1 point for telling about the feeling, plus 1 extra point for guessing the correct hand. (If you did not guess the correct hand, you still get a point for telling a time you experienced the feeling.) We will play a few rounds of the game, and I will choose a different Feeling-Word Square each time.

You can earn an extra point when you rate the intensity of the feeling. This means saying whether you experienced the feeling a tiny bit, a little, medium, a lot, or extremely. Hold up the number of fingers to show the intensity of the feeling. Use the Feeling Rating Scale and read the examples below to understand this better.

Feeling Rating Scale
5 fingers = extremely
4 fingers = a lot
3 fingers = medium
2 fingers = a little
1 finger = tiny bit

Example 1: Ali felt <u>scared</u> getting a needle (a shot) from the doctor. Ali is holding up <u>4 fingers</u> because Ali felt "<u>a lot</u>" scared.

Example 2: Ali felt <u>scared</u> when Ali woke up from a bad dream. Ali is holding up <u>2 fingers</u> to show that Ali felt "<u>a little</u>" scared.

At the end of the game, trade in points for a prize: 1–10 points = 1 prize; 11 or more points = 2 prizes.

Guess Which Hand
Feeling-Word Squares

HAPPY Something good happens	**SAD** Something upsets you	**ANGRY** You don't like what is happening	**SCARED** Something scary or dangerous is happening
WORRIED You are afraid something bad is going to happen	**BRAVE** You do something that's scary to do	**LONELY** You have nobody to be with	**SAFE** You know something bad won't happen
PROUD You feel good about something you do well	**GUILTY** You feel bad about something you did wrong	**FRUSTRATED** You try to do something but you can't do it	**LOVE** You care about someone a lot
JEALOUS Someone has something you want	**EXCITED** You are looking forward to something good happening	**KIND** You treat someone nicely	**CALM** You are relaxed

Air Hockey Feelings Game

The Air Hockey Feelings game will help you talk about feelings. We will take turns choosing one Feeling-Word Square. The first person to choose will crumple the Feeling-Word Square into a round wad (the puck) and place it in the center of the rink. To begin the game, we will both kneel down beside the hockey rink. We will each put a straw in our mouth and place the other end of the straw just behind the puck. At the count of three, we will both blow into our straws and try to move the puck toward the net at one end of the hockey rink. Once we have blown the puck into that net, we will blow it toward the other end, into the other net. (The nets are the spaces marked with the masking tape at each end of the hockey rink.) If the puck gets blown outside the hockey rink, place it back in the middle of the rink and begin again. This is cooperative air hockey, which means we're on the same team and we must work together to blow the puck from one end of the rink to the other. Once we have successfully blown the puck from one net into the other net, the person who chose the feeling word will uncrumple the wad of paper and read the feeling word out loud. We will then take turns telling a time we experienced that feeling. You get 1 point for telling about the feeling.

You earn an extra point when you rate the intensity of the feeling. This means saying whether you experienced the feeling a tiny bit, a little, medium, a lot, or extremely. Hold up the number of fingers to show the intensity of the feeling. Use the Feeling Rating Scale and read the examples below to understand this better.

Feeling Rating Scale
5 fingers = extremely
4 fingers = a lot
3 fingers = medium
2 fingers = a little
1 finger = tiny bit

Example 1: Ali felt scared getting a needle (a shot) from the doctor. Ali is holding up 4 fingers because Ali felt "a lot" scared.

Example 2: Ali felt scared when Ali woke up from a bad dream. Ali is holding up 2 fingers to show that Ali felt "a little" scared.

We will play several rounds of Air Hockey Feelings and use a new feeling-word square for each round. We'll set the timer at the beginning of each round and see how fast we can work together to blow the puck from one net to the other. At the end of the game, trade in points for a prize: 1–10 points = 1 prize; 11 or more points = 2 prizes.

Air Hockey Feelings Game
Air Hockey Rink

Use tape to make the rink. Begin by clearing a large space on the floor. To make the hockey rink, tape two pieces of masking tape along the floor (each piece of tape should be about 4 feet long, and placed about 2 feet apart.) Use tape to make the nets by placing tape at each end of the rink in the shape of a U. (Use the diagram as a guide. The dotted lines are the tape.) Alternatively, draw the hockey rink on a large piece of cardboard, poster board, or white board, and place it on the floor or on a table. Ensure there is ample space for two players to move around the hockey rink.

Air Hockey Rink
Diagram

Air Hockey Feelings Game
Feeling-Word Squares

HAPPY Something good happens	**SAD** Something upsets you	**ANGRY** You don't like what is happening	**SCARED** Something scary or dangerous is happening
WORRIED You are afraid something bad is going to happen	**BRAVE** You do something that's scary to do	**LONELY** You have nobody to be with	**SAFE** You know something bad won't happen
PROUD You feel good about something you do well	**GUILTY** You feel bad about something you did wrong	**FRUSTRATED** You try to do something but you can't do it	**LOVE** You care about someone a lot
JEALOUS Someone has something you want	**EXCITED** You are looking forward to something good happening	**KIND** You treat someone nicely	**CALM** You are relaxed

Practice Activity to Do at Home:
Talking About Feelings

Talking to your parent(s) about how you feel is a good way to get your feelings out and feel better. Each day, look at this Feeling Sheet and point to the feelings that you experienced that day. Describe in detail what happened and the different feelings you experienced.

HAPPY Something good happens	**SAD** Something upsets you	**ANGRY** You don't like what is happening	**SCARED** Something scary or dangerous is happening
WORRIED You are afraid something bad is going to happen	**BRAVE** You do something that's scary to do	**LONELY** You have nobody to be with	**SAFE** You know something bad won't happen
PROUD You feel good about something you do well	**GUILTY** You feel bad about something you did wrong	**FRUSTRATED** You try to do something but you can't do it	**LOVE** You care about someone a lot
JEALOUS Someone has something you want	**EXCITED** You are looking forward to something good happening	**KIND** You treat someone nicely	**CALM** You are relaxed

Information Sheet for Parents:
Feelings

Key Points

- It is important for children to develop an awareness of how they feel and to be able to talk about how they feel. It is also important for children to learn that feelings vary in intensity (e.g., feeling a little scared versus feeling a lot scared).

- Children who have a large vocabulary of names for feelings are better able to express their emotions using language, rather than inappropriate behaviors.

- Learning to identify and express feelings at this point in therapy will help prepare your child for tasks that will be introduced in later stages of therapy.

Tips

If you express your emotions in an open and healthy way, it will help your child express emotions in an open and healthy way. Here are some specific ways you can help your child:

- Label your emotions to help your child learn a "feelings vocabulary." For example, say, "I feel frustrated because this jar is so hard to open."

- Label your child's feelings and invite open discussion. For example, say, "You look sad right now. Tell me about your sad feelings."

- Normalize that everyone feels scared and worried at times but we can manage this distress. For example, say, "Even though I feel worried about going to this party because I don't know anybody, I know I will be fine and I will have fun."

- Provide regular opportunities for your child to talk with you about their feelings. When your child talks with you about their feelings, don't feel like you have to make it all better—simply listening to your child and validating their feelings is what your child needs most from you.

Section 6

Cognitive Coping

Children with anxiety have negative, irrational, or unhelpful thoughts and beliefs, which lead to heightened feelings of anxiety. Helping clients to understand the connection between thoughts, feelings, and behaviors (called the "cognitive triangle") and to replace unhelpful, anxious self-talk with helpful, calming self-talk, are key goals in cognitive behavioral therapy (CBT). More specifically, children learn to "replace negative or danger-oriented talk with self-talk that emphasizes coping ability, decreases worry, boosts self-confidence, and reinforces effort and success" (Wagner, 2005, p. 88). The activities in this chapter are playful and concrete to make the learning more accessible. Parents should be included in the session to help them learn the concepts.

Younger children (or children with cognitive delays) may have difficulty understanding the cognitive triangle. However, they can usually understand the basics of cognitive coping (e.g., thinking happy or calm thoughts can help us feel better). Children can be taught adaptive, coping self-statements. However, such positive self-statements must be adapted to the age of the child. Young children can be taught self-affirming statements that are linguistically and conceptually simple, such as "I am safe" or "I can do this" (Knell, 2006). Coping self-statements can be taught in therapy but should be modeled and reinforced by parents.

Bibliotherapy on cognitive coping can help reinforce concepts. Suggested books include *The Hyena Who Lost Her Laugh* (Lamb-Shapiro, 2000); *The Little Engine That Could* (Piper, 1930); and *Thinking About Thoughts* (Matlow, 2011).

Interventions

Letting the Butterflies Out of the Bag (page 74)
Ages: 6–12
Objective: Structure and limit pervasive worry
Supplies: Paper bag filled with butterfly worries completed in prior session, several copies of the butterfly outlines (see page 31), scissors, markers, timer
Advance Preparation:
Cut out the butterfly outlines. Copy the following guidelines onto a sheet of paper to give to the parents:

- Listen to your child's worries. Don't talk about yourself or offer any "me too" comments (e.g., "Yeah, I worry about that too").

- Don't try to make your child feel better or offer any advice to help make the worries go away.

- Encourage your child to talk more about worries (e.g., "Tell me more about your worries"; "How else does this worry you?"; "What else are you worried about?").

- If your child begins talking about anything good or positive, say, "Only talk about your worries, please."

- If your child runs out of worries, say, "Tell me again about those worries you talked about before."

Description:
Scheduling worry time is a stimulus control training technique that helps the client gain control over the frequency and timing of worry. This CBT strategy teaches the child to contain worry to a daily, designated time period, thereby freeing up the mind for other non-stressful thoughts and activities. The purpose of scheduling worry time is to: (1) Help the child externalize worries by getting them out in a structured, as opposed to random, way; (2) Enable the child to delay worrying until the scheduled time so worries can be compartmentalized; and (3) Help the child to see, over time, the repetitiveness and uselessness of the worries, as they typically will talk about the same worries over and over (Zucker, 2009). This activity is a continuation of Butterflies in My Stomach (from Section 2: Engagement and Assessment) and should be completed with the child and parents. It is essential to first meet with the parents (without the child) to prepare them for this activity. Explain to parents the rationale for the intervention and review the handout (*see* Advance Preparation, above). Role-play with the parents so they feel confident on ways to elicit worries from their child during worry time, and help them set limits on worry talk. Worry time should be done at home only after the parents and child are able to do it properly in session. Stress to the parents and child the importance of doing worry time at home for seven consecutive days. This intervention is for children who worry excessively and should only be considered for clients who need to structure and limit pervasive worry. It works best with clients who have demonstrated consistent follow-through with prior homework tasks. If, after seven days of doing worry time at home, the child has not made significant progress in limiting pervasive worry, explore this lack of progress in therapy. Lack of progress can usually be attributed to inconsistent or inappropriate use of the technique. (Note: Letting the Butterflies Out of the Bag is an original intervention, but the concept of worry time has been written about elsewhere.)

Jamie's Story (Chapter Four: Helpful Thoughts) (page 77)
Ages: 6–8
Objective: Learn positive coping statements; replace unhelpful thoughts with helpful thoughts
Supplies: Paper, markers, bag filled with small prizes
Description:
This chapter introduces clients to the concept of cognitive techniques aimed at correcting dysfunctional thoughts. Examples that most young children can easily understand and relate to are provided.

Helpful Thoughts (page 79)
Ages: 8–14
Objective: Learn the connection between thoughts, feelings, and behaviors; replace unhelpful thoughts with helpful thoughts
Supplies: Three sheets of 8.5 x 11-inch paper, marker, string or masking tape, scissors
Description:
This intervention teaches children concepts that might otherwise be difficult for them to grasp. Children typically respond well to the visual, active, and experiential aspect of this activity. Younger clients usually enjoy choosing and using an action to move along the giant floor triangle. If older clients find this aspect silly, they can omit choosing an action and simply walk normally around the triangle. A list of helpful thoughts is included for clients who have difficulty identifying positive coping statements. This list is intended as a guide and is for use at the therapist's discretion. At first glance, this intervention might seem overly complicated; however, the step-by-step instructions make it easy for children to understand and follow. The practitioner, child, and parents can obtain a clearer understanding of this activity by watching the Helpful Thoughts video on the author's YouTube channel (http://www.youtube.com/user/lowensteinliana). Teaching CBT skills to children via YouTube videos offers considerable intuitive appeal. Most children are familiar with YouTube and are likely to find this method of instruction quite captivating. Moreover, using a YouTube video involving another child to teach CBT skills incorporates the principles inherent to observational learning and offers the opportunity for a child to model the skills (Friedberg et al., 2000).

Bug Off (page 87)
Ages: 8–12
Objective: Replace unhelpful thoughts with helpful thoughts
Supplies: Several copies of the worry bugs, scissors, markers
Advance Preparation:
Cut out the worry bugs.
Description:
Externalization puts anxiety outside the client, and helps the client see the worry and its unhelpful messages from a different perspective. With this distance, the child can learn to move away from the worry and take back control (Wilson & Lyons, 2013). The Bug Off activity facilitates externalization and empowers the child to take control and get rid of their automatic anxious thoughts. The Helpful Thoughts activity (see above) should be completed in a session prior to this activity.

Willy's Worries and the Wise Wizard (page 90)
Ages: 8–12
Objective: Replace negative self-talk with positive self-talk
Description:
Most clients make negative, irrational, and self-defeating statements about themselves that often lead to heightened feelings of worthlessness and anxiety. It is important to help clients replace negative, self-defeating statements with positive, self-enhancing statements. Self-talk is a skill that children can use when they are feeling discouraged, angry, anxious, or afraid. Most children will relate to Willy, and will therefore be more receptive to learning how to replace negative self-talk with positive self-talk.

Letting the Butterflies Out of the Bag

This is the second part of the Butterflies in My Stomach activity that we started in an earlier session. This part of the activity will help you learn a technique to get control over your worries. Letting the Butterflies Out of the Bag is a strategy that will help you set a special time each day for "worry time," which will free up the rest of your day for more positive, helpful thoughts.

Read through the worries that you wrote before on paper butterflies. Use the blank paper butterflies to write down any more worries that you have (e.g., I'm worried about a math test I have this week; I'm worried about going to my friend's birthday party). Add these new worries to the bag. Cut out several extra paper butterflies and add them to the bag too, so you have blank ones to use when needed.

Set a timer for ten minutes. Spend ten minutes in the session talking with your parent(s) about your worries. For example, read each worry written on the paper butterflies, describe each worry, say why the situation makes you feel worried, and talk about the bad things that you think might happen. You have ten minutes to say whatever you want about your worries. During the ten-minute worry time, you must do the following:

Spend this entire time thinking and talking only about your worries. Do not think or talk about anything good or happy. Only think and talk about worries. Try to become anxious and uncomfortable during worry time, even though it may be hard and may not feel good. Keep talking and thinking about your worries until the ten minutes is over. If you run out of worries to talk about, repeat the same worries over and over.

During worry time, your parent(s) will listen to your worries and will help you talk more about worries. If you begin talking about anything good or positive, your parent(s) will say, "Only talk about your worries, please."

When the ten-minute timer goes off, you and your parent(s) must follow the steps below:

(1) Your parent(s) will say: "Worry time is over for today."
(2) You must immediately stop talking about your worries.
(3) Take three calming deep breaths.

Take your worry bag home. Your parent(s) will help you choose a specific time each day for worry time. This is the time when you can talk about your worries (butterflies), and let the butterflies out of the bag! Do worry time in a quiet, private place with no distractions or interruptions (e.g., TV, computer, and phones off; no interruptions from siblings or anyone else).

For this to work, you must do worry time for ten minutes for at least seven days in a row. And you must follow this <u>very important</u> rule:

If a worry bothers you at any other time of the day, you are not allowed to think or talk about it until worry time. You must imagine putting the worries (butterflies) back into the worry bag. It helps to say to yourself, "I'm not worrying about this now. I will worry about this during worry time." Your parent(s) will remind you of this very important rule. So, if you start talking about a worry or if you ask a worry question and it is not worry time, your parent(s) will say: "Put the butterfly (worry) back in your worry bag until it is time to let the butterflies (worries) out of the bag during worry time." If you ask a worry question and it is not worry time, your parent(s) will not answer your worry question. You might think your parent is being mean. You might get angry at your parent(s) for not letting you talk about your worries or for not answering your worry question. But sticking to this rule will help you.

At first, most kids find it really hard to wait until worry time to think and talk about worries. When it is worry time, they have lots of worries to talk about. But after a few days, most kids get bored talking about worries over and over again. Feeling bored is much better than feeling worried. But guess what? That's the point! After the seven days, you may find that you don't need the whole ten minutes to talk about worries. If that's the case, you can spend the ten minutes talking with your parent(s) about other things that are on your mind. You can change the name from Worry Time to Talk Time.

Practice Activity to Do at Home:
Letting the Butterflies Out of the Bag

Follow these rules for the next seven to ten days:

- Choose a specific time each day for worry time. (Make it around the same time each day, like at 5 p.m. Don't do it close to bedtime.)

- Do worry time in a quiet, private place with no distractions or interruptions (e.g., TV, computer, and phones off; no interruptions from siblings or anyone else). It's helpful to choose the same "worry chair" to sit in every time.

- Set a timer (or an alarm clock) for ten minutes. Spend the whole ten minutes talking with your parent(s) about your worries. Read each worry written on the paper butterflies. Describe each worry, say why the situation makes you feel worried, and talk about the bad things that you think might happen. Spend this entire time thinking and talking only about your worries. Do not think or talk about anything good or happy during this ten-minute worry time. Only think and talk about worries. Try to become anxious and uncomfortable during worry time. Keep talking and thinking about your worries until the ten minutes of worry time is over. If you run out of worries to talk about, repeat the same worries over and over.

During worry time, your parent(s) will listen to your worries and will help you talk more about worries.

When the ten-minute timer goes off:

(1) Your parent(s) will say: "Worry time is over for today."
(2) You must immediately stop talking about your worries.
(3) Take three calming deep breaths.
(4) Go do something else that will take your mind off your worries.

*** If a worry bothers you and it is not worry time, put the worry (butterfly) back in your worry bag until worry time, and say to yourself, "I don't need to worry about this now, I can worry about this later during worry time."

Jamie's Story
Chapter Four: Helpful Thoughts

Welcome back to the story!

Jamie came to therapy looking worried. Ana asked what was wrong. Jamie replied, "I have a soccer game later. What if I don't play good? What if everyone thinks I'm the worst player on the team?" Ana said, "Jamie, you are feeling worried because you are thinking worried thoughts. Worried thoughts are unhelpful thoughts because worried thoughts make you feel more worried. If you think calm, helpful thoughts, then you won't feel worried. If you think calm, helpful thoughts, then you will feel better. Today we're going to learn how to change unhelpful thoughts to helpful thoughts because this will help you feel better."

Is Jamie feeling worried about the soccer game because Jamie is thinking worried thoughts?

Are worried thoughts unhelpful thoughts because worried thoughts make you feel more worried?

If you think calm, helpful thoughts, will you feel better?

Ana said, "If you change unhelpful thoughts to helpful thoughts, it will make you feel better. Read the example below to see what I mean."

Situation: I have a soccer game.
Unhelpful Thoughts: What if I don't play good? What if everyone thinks I'm the worst player on the team?
These **unhelpful thoughts** make me feel **worried** and **upset**.
Helpful Thoughts: I'll do my best. I don't have to be the best player on the team.
These **helpful thoughts** make me feel **calmer** and **better**.

Ana said, "Thinking helpful thoughts will make you feel better. If you practice changing unhelpful thoughts to helpful thoughts you will get good at it. This will help you feel better!"

If you practice changing unhelpful thoughts to helpful thoughts will you get good at it and will this help you feel better?

Practice changing unhelpful thoughts to helpful thoughts. Draw a big happy face on a piece of paper. Turn the paper over and draw a big sad face on the other side. I am going to read the situations below out loud. Hold up the paper with the sad face when I say the unhelpful thought. Hold up the paper with the happy face when I say the helpful thought.

Situation: My favorite cereal is all gone.
Unhelpful Thought: I have nothing good to eat for breakfast.
Helpful Thought: There are other foods I like that I can eat for breakfast.

Situation: I have to get a needle (a shot) from the doctor.
Unhelpful Thought: It's too scary. I can't do this.
Helpful Thought: The needle will hurt for a bit, then I'll be okay. I can do this.

Situation: Mom/Dad are going out for dinner.
Unhelpful Thought: Mom/Dad will get hurt in a bad accident and won't come back.
Helpful Thought: Mom/Dad will be fine and will be back later.

Situation: My picture didn't turn out the way I wanted.
Unhelpful Thought: This is the worst drawing ever!
Helpful Thought: It doesn't have to look perfect.

Situation: It's my turn to read in front of the class.
Unhelpful Thought: I'll sound weird and everyone will laugh at me.
Helpful Thought: I'll be fine. I can do this.

Situation: I just heard a loud noise outside.
Unhelpful Thought: A robber must be breaking into our house!
Helpful Thought: It's probably just noise from the trees. I'm safe in my house.

Situation: There are gigantic green elephants with purple polka dots in the sky.
Unhelpful Thought: What if they fall from the sky and smush my house?
Helpful Thought: I don't have to worry about this because...elephants are not green with purple polka dots!

Helpful Thoughts

We all have thoughts in our head. Sometimes these thoughts are unhelpful and make us feel worried or upset (e.g., "I'm going to fail") and sometimes these thoughts are helpful and make us feel good (e.g., "I can do this"). Our thoughts make a difference to how we feel and what we do. This activity will help you understand this idea so you can learn to control worried, unhelpful thoughts and help yourself feel better. Follow the instructions below:

Make a giant floor triangle

Write the word THOUGHTS in large block letters on a sheet of paper. Write the words FEELINGS/BODY SENSATIONS in large block letters on a sheet of paper. Write the word BEHAVIORS in large block letters on a sheet of paper. Use the sheets marked THOUGHTS, FEELINGS/BODY SENSATIONS, and BEHAVIORS to make the shape of a triangle on the floor. Here's how: Place the sheet marked THOUGHTS at the top corner of the triangle on the floor. Place the sheet marked FEELINGS/BODY SENSATIONS at the bottom-right corner of the triangle on the floor, about six feet away from the THOUGHTS sheet. Place the sheet marked BEHAVIORS at the bottom-left corner of the triangle on the floor, about six feet away from the FEELINGS/BODY SENSATIONS sheet.

Connect the corners of the triangle using masking tape or string. Here's how: Use masking tape or string to "draw" a line on the floor from the sheet marked THOUGHTS to the sheet marked FEELINGS/BODY SENSATIONS. Do the same thing between the sheet marked FEELINGS/BODY SENSATIONS to the sheet marked BEHAVIORS and finally, from the sheet marked BEHAVIORS back to the sheet marked THOUGHTS. When you are finished, the masking tape or string should look like the outline of a triangle on the floor, like the diagram below.

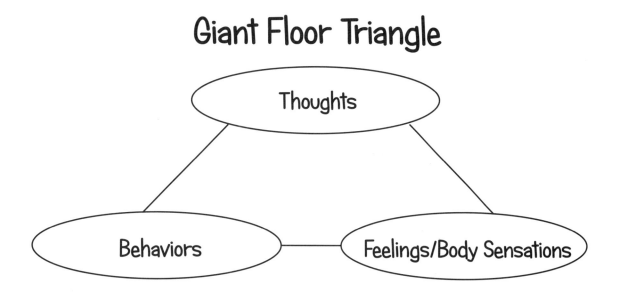

Giant Floor Triangle

Learn how to change unhelpful thoughts to helpful thoughts

Notice how thoughts, feelings/body sensations, and behaviors are all connected? Now let's talk about an example to help you understand how thoughts, feelings/body sensations, and behaviors are connected. Let's say you're afraid of spiders. You see a creepy crawly spider on the floor. Your thoughts in the situation are: *The spider is so creepy! It may crawl on me and that would be even creepier!* Thinking this makes you feel scared and yucky. The scared, yucky feelings make your heart pound faster and your body get tight and sweaty. Then you jump up on the chair so the creepy crawly spider can't crawl on you!

Walk to the word THOUGHTS at the top corner of the triangle. Repeat out loud your <u>thoughts</u> when you see the spider: *The spider is so creepy! It may crawl on me and that would be even creepier!*

Walk to the words FEELINGS/BODY SENSATIONS at the bottom-right corner of the triangle. Repeat out loud your <u>feelings and body sensations</u> in this situation: *Scared, yucky, heart pounding faster, body tight, and sweaty.*

Walk to the word BEHAVIORS at the bottom-left corner of the triangle. Repeat out loud your <u>behaviors</u> in this situation: *Jump up on the chair.*

Thinking a different thought can change how we feel and behave. When you see a spider and you change the thought to *It's just a tiny, harmless little thing; it can't hurt me,* then you feel calm and safe, and you are able to sit calmly in the chair.

Walk to the word THOUGHTS at the top corner of the triangle. Repeat out loud your <u>thoughts</u> this time when you see the spider: *It's just a tiny, harmless little thing; it can't hurt me.*

Walk to the words FEELINGS/BODY SENSATIONS at the bottom-right corner of the triangle. Repeat out loud your <u>feelings and body sensations</u> this time in this situation: *Calm and safe, relaxed body.*

Walk to the word BEHAVIORS at the bottom-left corner of the triangle. Repeat out loud your <u>behaviors</u> this time in this situation: *Able to sit calmly in the chair.*

Do your feelings and behaviors stay the same or change in this second example? How come?

Now let's play the Helpful Thoughts game to help us learn how <u>unhelpful</u> thoughts can make us feel worse and have a negative effect on what we do, and how <u>helpful</u> thoughts can help us cope better with situations.

Practice changing unhelpful thoughts to helpful thoughts

Look at the Action Cards and choose the one you like best (e.g., hop on right foot). This will be the action you use to move around the giant floor triangle. (If you prefer not to use an action, you can leave this part out and simply walk to the different parts of the giant floor triangle.) Read all of the Unhelpful Thoughts Cards and choose one. Read the chosen card aloud, and as you read it, move to the appropriate word on the giant triangle on the floor (THOUGHTS, FEELINGS/BODY SENSATIONS, or BEHAVIORS). Use your chosen action to move to the other two words in different corners of the triangle. (If you prefer, you can walk normally to the different corners.) At each corner of the triangle, stop and read the corresponding part of the Unhelpful Thoughts Card.

Play the game again, but this time, use the Helpful Thoughts Card. Read the chosen card aloud, and as you read it, move to the appropriate word on the giant triangle on the floor (THOUGHTS, FEELINGS/BODY SENSATIONS, or BEHAVIORS). Use your chosen action to move to the other two words in different corners of the triangle. (If you prefer, you can walk normally to the two words in different corners of the triangle.) At each corner of the triangle, stop and read the corresponding part on the Helpful Thoughts Card.

Make up your own situation card (a time you felt worried). Stand on the word THOUGHTS on the giant floor triangle and say an unhelpful thought you might have in this situation. As you move to the FEELINGS/BODY SENSATIONS and BEHAVIORS spaces on the giant floor triangle, add the feelings, body sensations, and behaviors you would have in this situation.

Go back and stand on the word THOUGHTS on the giant floor triangle. This time, say a helpful thought that could help you cope or feel better in this situation. (If you are having a hard time coming up with a helpful thought, look at the Helpful Thoughts on page 85 to get some ideas.) As you move to the FEELINGS/BODY SENSATIONS and BEHAVIORS spaces on the giant floor triangle, add the feelings, body sensations, and behaviors you would have when you think this helpful thought.

You can make yourself feel better by thinking helpful thoughts, but it takes practice. When you get worried or upset, notice any unhelpful thoughts you had in the situation. Then try to replace the unhelpful thoughts with helpful thoughts. Thinking helpful thoughts will control worried, upset feelings, and help you feel better.

Action Cards

HOP ON YOUR LEFT FOOT	HOP ON YOUR RIGHT FOOT
STOMP AS YOU WALK	WALK IN SLOW MOTION
MARCH LIKE A SOLDIER	MAKE UP YOUR OWN ACTION

Unhelpful Thoughts Cards

-1- **Parent is late** **picking you up** Unhelpful Thoughts: Something awful happened to my parent Feelings/Body Sensations: Worried/Heart pounding, sore tummy Behaviors: Crying, looking around for parent	**-2-** **You're invited to** **a friend's party** Unhelpful Thoughts: I won't know anyone; I'll have a terrible time Feelings/Body Sensations: Worried, scared/Sore tummy, tight muscles Behaviors: Cling to parent, refuse to go to the party
-3- **You're doing a spelling** **test at school** Unhelpful Thoughts: I can't do this; it's too hard; I'll fail Feelings/Body Sensations: Worried, hopeless/Heart pounding, sweating Behaviors: Cry, run out of the classroom	**-4-** **You wake up from** **a scary dream** Unhelpful Thoughts: The monster's going to get me Feelings/Body Sensations: Scared, unsafe/Heart pounding, sweating Behaviors: Cry, run to parents' bed

Helpful Thoughts Cards

-1- **Parent is late picking you up** **Helpful Thoughts:** My parent is fine and will be here soon **New Feelings/Body Sensations:** Calm/Relaxed body **Behaviors:** Do something fun while waiting for parent	-2- **You're invited to a friend's party** **Helpful Thoughts:** I'm nervous but I can still have fun **New Feelings/Body Sensations:** Happy, excited/Calm tummy, relaxed body **Behaviors:** Go to the party and enjoy the time there
-3- **You're doing a spelling test at school** **Helpful Thoughts:** I studied for this test and I'll try my best **New Feelings/Body Sensations:** Calm, confident/Relaxed body **Behaviors:** Complete the test	-4- **You wake up from a scary dream** **Helpful Thoughts:** It's not real; it's just a dream; I'm safe **New Feelings/Body Sensations:** Safe, calm/Relaxed body **Behaviors:** Go back to sleep

Helpful Thoughts

THIS ISN'T EASY BUT I CAN TRY MY BEST

I'VE GOTTEN THROUGH DIFFICULT TIMES BEFORE, I CAN
GET THROUGH THIS

EVEN THOUGH I FEEL WORRIED I CAN STILL HAVE FUN

I DON'T HAVE TO BE PERFECT

MAKING MISTAKES IS PART OF LEARNING

IT DIDN'T GO THE WAY I WANTED BUT I STILL HAD FUN

THIS IS BOTHERING ME BUT IT'S NOT DANGEROUS

I'M NERVOUS BUT I CAN HANDLE IT

I CAN CHOOSE TO BE BRAVE

Practice Activity to Do at Home:
Helpful Thoughts

When you get worried or upset, notice any unhelpful thoughts you had in the situation. Then try to replace the unhelpful thoughts with helpful thoughts.

Anxious or upsetting situation: _____

Unhelpful thoughts:

_____

_____

Feelings/Body Sensations: _____

Helpful thoughts:

_____

_____

New Feelings/Body Sensations: _____

Anxious or upsetting situation: _____

Unhelpful thoughts:

_____

_____

Feelings/Body Sensations: _____

Helpful thoughts:

_____

_____

New Feelings/Body Sensations: _____

Anxious or upsetting situation: _____

Unhelpful thoughts:

_____

_____

Feelings/Body Sensations: _____

Helpful thoughts:

_____

_____

New Feelings/Body Sensations: _____

Bug Off!

The Helpful Thoughts game taught you how to change unhelpful thoughts to helpful thoughts. This activity will help you practice. Write an unhelpful thought (a worry thought) on each worry bug. This should be a thought that makes you feel worried and anxious. Below are some examples:

I'm going to fail my test tomorrow.

What if something bad happens to my parent?

What if everyone laughs at me?

That noise must be a robber!

The dog is going to attack me!

Pretend these worry bugs are flying around your head making you feel more and more worried. They are such a nuisance! You can make them go away. Here's how:

Stand facing me, with about four feet between us. I will read the unhelpful worry thought written on one of the worry bugs, crumple it, and throw it toward you. Swat it away! Then say a helpful thought to replace the unhelpful worry thought. This will make the worry bug stay away. Repeat these steps until you have gotten rid of all the worry bugs.

Doing this activity may not make all your worries go away, but it can remind you to think helpful thoughts. So, when a worry bug (unhelpful worry thought) is buzzing around your head, pretend to swat it away. Come up with a helpful thought to make it stay away!

Bug Off!
Worry Bugs

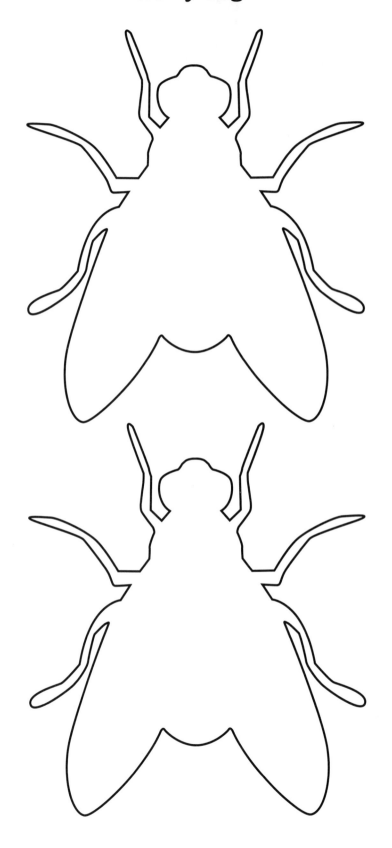

Practice Activity to Do at Home:
Bug Off!

When a worry bug (unhelpful worry thought) is buzzing around your head, pretend to swat it away. Come up with a helpful thought to make it stay away!

Worry that's bugging me: _____

Unhelpful thought:

_____

_____

Helpful thought:

_____

_____

Worry that's bugging me: _____

Unhelpful thought:

_____

_____

Helpful thought:

_____

_____

Worry that's bugging me: _____

Unhelpful thought:

_____

_____

Helpful thought:

_____

_____

Willy's Worries and the Wise Wizard

Most people carry on silent conversations with themselves; this is called self-talk. We tend to repeat the same messages to ourselves over and over, and soon, we come to believe these silent messages. If this self-talk is negative, then it makes us feel bad. For example, if I were to think to myself, *I cannot do anything right,* I would soon believe this. I would feel bad, and then I would probably not do as well. But if self-talk is positive, it makes us feel happier. For example, if I were to think to myself, *I can try my best,* I would feel calmer and happier.

The story, Willy's Worries and the Wise Wizard, will help you learn more about this. Read the story then answer the questions below.

Did Willy's worries make it hard for him to feel happy and to have fun?

What special power does Willy (and each and every person) have? How does this special power help Willy?

Write down a negative thought, then change it to a positive thought:

Story
Willy's Worries and the Wise Wizard

This is a story about a boy named Willy. His real name is William, but most people call him Willy. Willy was a typical kid in a lot of ways; he liked to play computer games and ride his bike, and he preferred dessert to eating vegetables! But Willy had a big problem. Willy worried a lot! He worried about things over and over. He worried so much he often got stomachaches. His worries made it hard for him to feel happy and to have fun.

One night as he lay in bed trying to fall asleep, he kept worrying about his upcoming soccer game. He worried he would play terribly and that all the kids on his team would make fun of him. This worry made his stomach hurt. Then he saw a spider on the wall—he was afraid of spiders! He buried himself under his blanket, shaking with fear. He could feel his heart pounding fast, and he became hot and sweaty.

After a while, Willy finally fell asleep. He dreamed the most wonderful dream—that he had magical powers and could make wishes come true! So, he wished to be the best soccer player on his team, and he wished there were no spiders in the world—and poof! His wishes came true! He felt so happy! But then something startled him, and he woke up and realized it was just a dream. He felt so awful. He buried himself under his blanket and cried. He lay there for a long time, and after a while, he fell asleep again. This time, he dreamed that a wizard came to him—a very old, wise wizard named Waldorf. He had a long white beard, and he wore a long purple cape with bright yellow shiny stars on it, and a tall pointy hat to match. But he did not have a magic wand.

"You can't be a real wizard," said Willy, "because you do not have a magic wand."

"Oh, but you see, my boy, I do not need a magic wand, for I have discovered a special power that does not require any magic."

"What kind of special power?" asked Willy.

"Well," replied Waldorf the Wizard, "it is a special power that will bring you happiness. It is the power to think positive thoughts."

"Huh? What do you mean?" asked Willy.
"Well, instead of thinking negative thoughts, think positive thoughts. And if you think positive thoughts, this will bring you happiness."

"I wish I had that special power," said Willy.

"Ah, but you do have this special power," replied Waldorf. "In fact, each and every person has this special power. They just have to use it."

"So you mean I have this special power?" asked Willy.

"Yes! I'll show you what I mean. First, think of a negative thought."

"Well," said Willy, "I have a soccer game tomorrow. I'm worried I'm going to play terribly and all the kids on my team will make fun of me."

"And how do you feel when you think this?"

"I feel upset and worried," replied Willy. "Now, change that negative thought into a positive thought."

"Well, let's see. I don't have to be the best soccer player on my team. I can try my hardest and I can have fun."

"How do you feel now, as you think these positive thoughts?"

"Now I feel excited to play soccer. I feel much happier!" replied Willy with a smile on his face.

"You see Willy…You have the power to think positive, and if you choose to use this power, you will feel happier!"

Just then, something startled Willy, and he woke up from his dream. He thought about his soccer game tomorrow. He thought to himself, "I'm going to try my best and have fun." Then he realized he didn't feel worried about soccer. In fact, he felt happy and excited about his game. Just then, he saw that same spider on his wall. Instead of burying himself under his blanket feeling scared, he thought to himself, "It's just a tiny, harmless little thing. It can't hurt me." Thinking this made the scared feelings disappear. "Wow!" he thought to himself, "I do have a special power!"

Practice Activity to Do at Home:
Positive Thoughts

When a negative thought pops into your head, change it to a positive thought. If you practice this every day, you will soon become a positive thinker and you will feel happier!

Anxious or upsetting situation: _____

Negative thought: _____

Positive thought: _____

Anxious or upsetting situation: _____

Negative thought: _____

Positive thought: _____

Anxious or upsetting situation: _____

Negative thought: _____

Positive thought: _____

Anxious or upsetting situation: _____

Negative thought: _____

Positive thought: _____

Anxious or upsetting situation: _____

Negative thought: _____

Positive thought: _____

Anxious or upsetting situation: _____

Negative thought: _____

Positive thought: _____

Information Sheet for Parents:
Helpful Thoughts

Key Points

- The way we think affects the way we feel and behave. If we think unhelpful thoughts, this generally makes us feel bad. Replacing unhelpful thoughts with helpful thoughts enables us to feel better and to respond to situations in a better way.

- If you master the skill of replacing unhelpful thoughts with helpful thoughts, you will be able to help your child do this too.

- Learning to replace unhelpful worry thoughts with helpful thoughts takes practice, but it is an important step to managing anxiety.

Tips

- Give praise whenever your child is successful at thinking helpful thoughts (e.g., "You just came up with a really positive way of thinking about that, way to go!").

- Anxious children attempt to feel less anxious by seeking reassurance from their parents. According to Reid Wilson and Lynn Lyons, authors of *Anxious Kids, Anxious Parents*, reassuring your child is often an unhelpful response as it does not help your child to manage thoughts and feelings. Instead of offering reassurance, prompt your child to replace unhelpful thoughts with helpful thoughts. Below is an example:

    Child: I'm scared to sleep in my own room.

    (Less helpful) Parent offering reassurance: You don't need to be scared to sleep in your own room. We already checked under the bed and in the closet and there are no monsters in here. If you need me, just call, but you'll be fine.

    (More helpful) Parent prompting child to use coping strategy: That sounds like an unhelpful worry thought. What's a helpful thought you can think instead?

    In the example above, prompting the child to replace the unhelpful worry thought with a helpful thought is a more effective way of coping.

Section 7

Exposure

Gradual exposure is a cognitive behavioral intervention designed to gradually overcome dysfunctional avoidance and thereby allow the child to regain optimal functioning. Through an exposure plan, the child approaches avoided situations and tests the reality of the fear. The goal of exposure is to "help the child realize that the feared outcome usually does not occur in the given situation, and even if it does happen, the anxiety will dissipate over time" (Pincus et al., 2011, p. 220). *In vivo* exposure refers to directly encountering the feared situation in real life. *Imaginal* exposure involves picturing oneself approaching the feared situation.

The process and benefits of gradual exposure should have been explained to the parents and child at the outset of therapy. However, it is important to reiterate this information at this stage in treatment. It is particularly helpful to make clear that when the exposure plan is done correctly, anxiety *always* goes down. The activities in this chapter include components that help explain the steps and benefits of gradual exposure.

The practitioner, parents, and child work together to develop the exposure plan. Children who have many different fears will create several exposure plans. Each exposure plan should contain items that go together and relate to the same overall fear. For example, the client might have one exposure plan for various fears related to separation anxiety, and another to cope with a fear of injections.

The first step to creating an exposure plan is to develop a list of feared situations. (The client may have already done this via the Butterflies in My Stomach activity in Section 2: Engagement and Assessment.) The following question can elicit the list of fears: "What would you like to do that you can't easily do now because you're too scared or worried?" If the child feels embarrassed to make the list of fears, it can be helpful to normalize by stating how common anxiety is in children (Zucker, 2009).

Once the list of feared situations has been developed, one is chosen to begin working on. It is best to choose a significant feared situation but not the hardest one. A plan is then created for the child to gradually get used to the feared situation so that each step is tolerable. Rather than prescribing and/or assigning exposure exercises to the child, it is better to enlist the child as co-engineer (Friedberg et al., 2009; Podell et al., 2010). This empowers the child to take charge of overcoming fears. The practitioner can offer input to ensure each step on the exposure plan is specific and doable, with details of time to be spent, the location, and what is to be achieved. As well, the practitioner needs to ensure that the steps are listed in an appropriately graded manner, from easiest to hardest.

The parents must be provided with ample guidance on ways they can support the child during the implementation of the exposure plan. (The Information Sheet for Parents at the end of this chapter provides a number of suggestions.) A schedule for implementing the plan can be discussed with the clients that takes into account frequent, consistent times to work on it.

During an exposure, the child does not use relaxation techniques, as these strategies can interfere with the process. The goal of gradual exposure is for the child to experience anxiety, become habituated to the feeling, and realize that it is tolerable. The child self-monitors and rates the level of distress before and after each exposure. For habituation to occur, the child "must continue with exposure and remain in the feared situation until anxiety peaks and begins to decline" (Wagner, 2005, p. 92). The goal is to prolong exposure to the point that the level of anxiety decreases by roughly 50% (Beidel & Turner, 2006).

Helping the child to emotionally engage for appropriately prolonged periods during exposures will facilitate habituation. If the child is having difficulty being emotionally engaged during the exposure, the parent can ask, "What feels scary to you right now?" or "What do you see or hear that is scaring you?" (adapted from Friedberg et al., 2009; Hembree, 2003). Brief, nonintrusive questions are best so the child does not get distracted. The practitioner can role-play with parents to help them become more comfortable with the process.

If the client is resistant to the gradual exposure plan, it is important to assess the underlying cause. For instance, the client may not feel safe enough with the practitioner to proceed with this treatment component, or the resistance may be reflective of the client's need to continue to avoid feared situations. The practitioner response will depend on the individual situation. Ensuring the client feels engaged and empowered during sessions is a critical element to the progress of therapy. If the client's resistance to the gradual exposure plan is due to avoidance and anxiety, the practitioner can employ various strategies such as:

- Explore the child's fear (e.g., "What are you worried might happen if you do this step?")

- Ask questions that will help the child see the benefits of completing the exposure plan (e.g., "How will your life be easier or more fun if you get over this fear?")

- Give the child appropriate options and choices throughout the plan (e.g., "What's a step you think you could do?" "When would you like to try this again?")

- Combine validation with encouragement (e.g., "I know this seems scary to you but I also know you can do this")

- Help the child challenge and correct unhelpful thoughts that are perpetuating feelings of anxiety

- Slow down the pace or create smaller steps (e.g., "Let's slow it down and together figure out the next step")

- Suggest playful imaginal exposure options to try first, such as drawing the feared situation in detail or enacting it with puppets or figurines

- Set up the exposure exercises as experiments (e.g., "Let's do an experiment to find out if you can prove that nothing bad or dangerous happens when you sleep in your bed with all the lights off")

- Ask the child to imagine giving advice to a friend (e.g., "If your friend was afraid of dogs, what advice would you give to help your friend overcome this fear?"). Younger children might imagine their favorite superhero offering them words of encouragement

- Consider offering small rewards for successful completion of each step on the exposure plan and make sure the rewards are desirable

Most children want to get over their fear; they just need help to do it. However, sometimes a child lacks the motivation to change. If this is the case, possible reasons underlying the lack of motivation should be explored. For example, perhaps the child gets more attention or nurturing from parents when distressed and does not want to give this up. Or the child might resist going to a friend's sleepover because they will miss out on a fun family outing.

In some cases, the parent is the source of resistance. For example, the parent's level of anxiety may be blocking the child's progress. Or the parent has a need to infantilize the child rather than encouraging the child's independence. Family dysfunction might also be the source of the child's resistance. For instance, a child might insist on sleeping in the parents' bed as an attempt to protect one parent from the other's abusive behavior. Pincus (2012) suggests figuring out the function of the child's resistant behavior by determining what the child might be gaining by staying afraid or what might be going on in the family system that is sustaining the child's fear.

Schools often put into place accommodations for anxious children, such as permitting the child to call home when feeling highly anxious, allowing the child to present an oral report to the teacher alone rather than to the whole class, and extending time on tests. These accommodations maintain the child's anxiety in the long-term. While accommodations may be helpful initially, an appropriate weaning-off plan is required. If the child's fears are interfering with school functioning, make sure to involve the child's teacher in supporting the exposure plan.

The practitioner may inadvertently impede the child's progress on the exposure plan. Practitioner fears about exposure include: lack of tolerance for negative affect; fears about managing the child's distress; reluctance to push the client; and concern that the exposure plan will backfire (Wagner, 2005). The practitioner may also lack skill in designing an appropriate exposure plan. It cannot be overstated that practitioners must have proper training and experience in exposure therapy for childhood anxiety prior to implementing this treatment component.

Interventions

Jamie's Story (Chapter Five: Facing Fears) (page 100)
Ages: 6–10
Objective: Explain benefits of and prepare client for gradual exposure
Supplies: Bag filled with small prizes
Description:
The purpose of this chapter of the story is to introduce the concept of gradual exposure, to address possible resistance to facing fears, and to motivate the child to work on an exposure plan. This story prepares children for gradual exposure, and is intended for use with younger clients prior to using the Picture It Poster.

Picture It Poster (page 102)
Ages: 6–12
Objective: Face feared situation with minimal anxiety
Supplies: Large sheet of paper, 5 x 3-inch index cards (or paper cut into 5 x 3-inch pieces), markers, scissors, glue or tape, copies of the tracking sheet
Description:
This activity engages the child in the development and implementation of a gradual exposure plan. It may require two sessions to complete. Younger children will need more input from parent and therapist. The concept of earning a reward for successful completion of the exposure plan is discussed at the outset of the activity as a way to motivate the client. The child creates a poster with drawings of the first and last steps of the exposure plan. This makes the exposure plan more concrete and manageable. The drawing part of this activity should not take longer than ten minutes. Some children might need prompts to move along quicker or to simplify their drawings. A tracking sheet is included to help the child rate feelings of distress before and after each exposure exercise. There is a sample to help the child understand how to complete it. (Note that there are two different tracking forms. The version for older children includes questions to help the client identify and replace unrealistic thought patterns.) Prior to doing the Picture It Poster with the child (and their parents), meet with parents without the child to explain gradual exposure, review the activity, and coach them on ways they can guide their child through the exposure exercises. The parent information sheet can be reviewed in session, as it contains detailed tips.

Play Clay Role-Play (page 111)

Ages: 6–9
Objective: Articulate readiness to face feared situation
Supplies: Ready-made clay or ingredients for homemade clay (bowl, spoon, flour, salt, vegetable oil, water, food coloring, garbage bag, tape)
Description:

This role-play is an *imaginal* exposure technique. It should be completed after the child has created an exposure plan (e.g., created the Picture It Poster). The role-play is an interim step to ready the child and parent for *in vivo* exposures. The Play Clay Role-Play "encourages desensitization and builds on a child's natural competencies" (Goodyear-Brown, 2010, p. 125). The sample role-play script illustrates for the parent key skills such as: encouraging the child through empathy, eliciting the fear rating, facilitating habituation, and praising the child's efforts. Additionally, the script helps the child better understand the process and benefits of exposure. Most children will enjoy making their own clay, but if this is not possible then store-bought clay can be used. Some clients will need guidance as they perform the role-play. The practitioner can take on the role of "director" to intervene at appropriate times during the role-play. After the role-play, process questions can emphasize learning points such as: "Do kids sometimes feel scared when they're about to do a new step from their Picture It Poster?" "Does facing a fear a little at a time, step by step, make it easier to get rid of a fear?" "When kids stick with it long enough (or do the scary thing a few times) does it always make their really scared feelings go away?"

Best Friend Role-Play (page 114)

Ages: 9–14
Objective: Articulate readiness to face feared situation
Description:

This role-play is an interim step to ready the client for *in vivo* exposures. The intervention facilitates a better understanding of the process and benefits of gradual exposure. As well, it reinforces that avoidance is not an effective coping strategy, and it offers a hopeful message that if clients persevere, they can overcome their fear. After the role-play, the discussion can help the client further accept that gradual exposure and habituation are the necessary tools for overcoming anxiety.

Jamie's Story
Chapter Five: Facing Fears

Welcome back to the story!

Jamie was excited to see Ana to tell her what had happened. Jamie said, "I was watching a movie on TV and at first I really liked it because it was so funny. But then the movie got really, really scary! Instead of turning off the TV I did Cookie Breathing to get calm. Then I said to myself, 'It's not real, it's just a movie.' This made the scared, worried feelings go away." Ana said, "Wow, Jamie! You are learning so much in therapy. You are learning ways to cope better with scared, worried feelings. That's a hard thing to learn and I hope you feel proud of this." "I do feel proud!" replied Jamie with a big smile.

Did Jamie cope with the scary movie by doing Cookie Breathing to get calm?

Does Jamie feel proud about learning ways to cope better with scared worried feelings?

Ana said, "Jamie, you have learned so much in therapy already. I know you're ready to do the next part—to face your fears. Facing fears means doing things that worry or scare you." Jamie interrupted Ana and said, "I don't want to do things that worry or scare me! I don't want to face my fears. It's too hard and scary!" Ana said, "Don't worry. We will make a plan to face fears a little at a time so it won't be too hard and it won't be too scary. Facing your fears a little at a time will make the really scared feelings go away. Lots of other kids have found that facing their fears a little at a time has made their really scared feelings go away, and this has made them feel so much calmer and happier."

Does facing fears mean doing things that make you feel worried or scared?

Does facing a fear a little at a time make the really scared feelings go away?

Have lots of other kids found that facing their fears a little at a time made their really scared feelings go away?

Ana said, "Jamie, we're going to make a plan to help you face your fears. I know you're nervous about this idea, so let me give you an example to help you understand this better. I worked with a child who was afraid to stay at a friend's house without their Mom there. Together, we came up with this step-by-step plan:

<u>Step 1 (easiest step)</u>: Go to friend's house for one hour during the day; Mom stays in another room.

<u>Step 2</u>: Go to friend's house for one hour during the day; Mom leaves for 15 minutes.

<u>Step 3</u>: Go to friend's house for two hours during the day; Mom leaves for 30 minutes.

<u>Step 4</u>: Get dropped off by Mom at friend's house; play there for 30 minutes.

<u>Step 5</u>: Get dropped off by Mom at friend's house; play there for one hour.

<u>Step 6</u>: Get dropped off by Mom at friend's house; play, then have dinner there; stay for three hours.

<u>Step 7</u>: Get dropped off by Mom at another friend's house; play there for one hour.

<u>Step 8</u>: Get dropped off by Mom at another friend's house; play, then have dinner there; stay for three hours.

<u>Step 9</u>: Sleep over at friend's house; call Mom two times before bed.

<u>Step 10 (hardest step)</u>: Sleep over at friend's house; call Mom once to say goodnight.

Ana said, "Notice that each step is small and he started with an easy step. As he was doing each step, he realized that nothing bad was going to happen. This made it easier for him to handle the situation. Once he was able to feel safe and okay doing the step, it was time to move on to the next step. Facing this fear a little at a time, step by step, helped him to get rid of these really scared feelings. Eventually, he got to the last step and was able to sleep over at a friend's house—and he no longer felt scared doing this! He was able to have fun at friends' houses, and at sleepovers and birthday parties. This made him so so so much happier! I know you want to be happier and have more fun too. And I know you are ready to begin to face fears." Jamie realized Ana was right—Jamie wanted to be happier. Jamie wanted to have more fun. So Jamie was ready to begin to face fears.

Is Jamie ready to begin to face fears?

Does facing a fear a little at a time, step by step, make it easier to get rid of really scared feelings?

Talk with your therapist/parent(s) and decide together on a fear that you want to get rid of. (Don't worry: You won't be working on facing this fear today. You are just writing down the fear you want to get rid of.)

Will getting rid of this fear help you feel happier?

Who are the adults who will help and support you to face your fears?

Picture It Poster

Most kids try to avoid (stay away from) the things that make them feel scared. But doing this isn't a good solution for a few reasons: first, it may stop you from doing activities you could enjoy; and second, fears have a way of creeping into your life over and over, and keeping you scared and unhappy if they are not dealt with. For example, if you are afraid of dogs, you might stay away from the park to avoid seeing dogs. Staying away from the park would stop you from having fun. And a lot of people have dogs, so you can't avoid them forever! Getting over your really scared feelings is a much better solution.

One way to get over really scared feelings is to face them a little at a time. Today we're going to make a plan to help you get over really scared feelings. Most kids actually want to get over really scared feelings, but they're not sure how to do it. We'll work together to develop a plan to help you get over really scared feelings. Follow the directions below.

(1) We're going to make a step-by-step plan to help you get over a big fear. But first, talk with your parent(s) and decide together on a reward you will get when you complete the last step of this plan. It should be something you really want that will help you celebrate your achievement of getting over a big fear! (It cannot be too expensive and your parent(s) must agree on it.)

Reward I'll get when I complete the last step of the plan: _____

(2) Make a list of fears (things you are afraid to do). Then choose from this list a fear you want to get rid of. If you have more than one fear, talk with your parent(s) and therapist about which one to start working on. Examples of fears include: petting a dog, sleeping in my own bed, using a public toilet, staying overnight at a friend's house.

Fear I want to get rid of: _____

(3) There are lots of good reasons for getting over your fear. Check off the ones below that apply to you (you can check off more than one):

____ Having this fear makes me feel scared a lot. I want to feel calmer and happier.
____ Having this fear often makes my body feel tense or sick. I want to feel better.
____ Having this fear makes me feel weird or different. I want to feel better about myself.
____ Having this fear keeps me from enjoying certain activities. I want to have more fun.

(4) Imagine a staircase starting with the first step at the bottom, the last step at the top, and a bunch of steps in between. Each step on the staircase is an action you will do to get over your scary situation. The steps go from least scary (at the bottom) to most scary (at the top). (See the sample Picture It Poster on page 106). Talk with your therapist and parent(s) and decide together on the first action you will do to begin to get over your fear. This first action should be something that is *easy* to do. This will be your first step at the bottom of the staircase. (Your therapist will help you write the step in a way that makes it specific and doable.) Your therapist will give you an index card or a piece of paper. Use it to draw a picture to show what you will do for your first step. Draw a simple, quick picture. Under the picture, write what you are doing (for example, "looking at pictures of dogs").

(5) Talk with your therapist and parent(s) and decide together on the last thing (the scariest action) you need to do to get over this fear. This will be your last step at the top of the staircase. Helpful hint: The last step is the goal you want to achieve (for example, pet a dog). (Your therapist will help you write the step in a way that makes it specific and doable.) Your therapist will give you an index card or a piece of paper. Use it to draw a picture to show what you will do for your last step. Draw a simple, quick picture. Under the picture, write what you are doing (for example, "petting a dog"). If drawing a picture to show what you will do for your last step is too scary right now, write it or ask your parent to write it on the index card. You can draw the picture of your last step later when you are ready.

(6) Talk with your therapist and parent(s) and decide together on the other things you will do to get over this fear. These will be the middle steps between your first step and your last step. Middle steps are actions that are between a little and very scary. The middle steps should be listed in order from easiest to hardest. (Your therapist will help you write the steps in a way that makes them specific, doable, and gradual.) If you are having trouble coming up with middle steps, think of things that make it easier or harder for you to do. One example is the length of time you might do a certain step (for example, holding a dog's leash for 30 seconds is less scary than holding a dog's leash for three minutes). Another example might be having your parent's help (for example, watching dogs from far away while holding your parent's hand is less scary than watching dogs from far away without holding your parent's hand). Write on a separate index card what you will do for each middle step. Write in pencil in case you want to make changes to the steps later.

(7) Place the index cards onto a large sheet of paper to form a staircase, starting with the picture of your first step at the bottom, then the index cards with each middle step written on them, then the picture of your last step at the top. Once the index cards are arranged on the sheet of paper, tape them down. (Leave room at the top for one index card.)

(8) Draw a simple, quick picture on an index card of yourself getting the reward after you have completed the last step. Glue this drawing at the top of your Picture It Poster, after the last step.

(9) Read the encouraging statements below. Check off the ones that will help you get started with the first step on your Picture It Poster. If you'd like, you can choose your favorite statements from the list below and write them on your Picture It Poster.

___ I am choosing to be brave.
___ I can do this.
___ I'm going to feel scared at first, and then it will be okay.
___ I'm willing to try hard because I want to overcome this fear.
___ My life will be happier once I get over these really scared feelings.
___ I must face my fear so I can get rid of it once and for all!

(10) When you begin each step, you will feel scared and uncomfortable at first. You will show how scared you feel by holding up fingers (see the Finger Fear Rating chart below). If you keep doing the step, you will soon realize that you are not in any danger and you can handle it. You will feel less and less scared. You'll keep doing the step until your fear number goes down one or two fingers. If your fear number is still at 5, 4, or 3, then repeat the step until your fear number is 2, 1, or 0. Move to the next step only when you feel ready. You will know you are ready because your fear number will be 2, 1, or 0. Remember, doing the steps will eventually make the really scared feelings go away! Think about doing the first step on your Picture It Poster. Show with your fingers how scared you feel as you think about doing this first step.

Finger Fear Rating:
5 fingers = extremely scared
4 fingers = a lot scared
3 fingers = medium scared
2 fingers = a little scared
1 finger = tiny bit scared
0 fingers = not scared

(11) Review the tracking sheet with your parent(s) and therapist so you know how to fill it in when you are ready to begin the first step on your Picture It Poster. (There is a sample tracking sheet for you to look at to help you learn how to fill this in.) You will get copies of the tracking sheet so you can fill out a separate one each time you start a new step on your Picture It Poster. Make sure you know which parts to fill out before you start a step, and which parts to fill out after you complete a step. Your parent can help you fill it out. Don't fill out the tracking sheet while you are doing a step. It is important that your full attention is on facing your fear, and the tracking sheet should not distract you.

(12) Make an agreement: "I am willing to work on facing my fear of _____
_____. I know facing this fear will make me feel scared and uncomfortable at first. But I understand that I will face this fear a little at a time and, eventually, the really scared feelings will go away. Once I complete the last step, I will be really excited to get my reward, which is _____."

(13) Talk with your parent(s) about when, where, and how you are going to work on your first few steps. It can help to make a schedule of what you are going to do and when you are going to do it. Planning ahead like this will help you feel in control. Doing all the steps may take days or even weeks.

Picture It Poster Reminders

❖ Do each of the steps one by one, starting with your <u>first step</u>, then each <u>middle step</u>, then your <u>last step</u>. Doing all the steps may take days or even weeks.

❖ Keep doing the step until your fear number goes down one or two fingers. If your fear number is still at 5, 4, or 3, repeat the step until your fear number is 2, 1, or 0. Move to the next step only when you feel ready. You will know you are ready because your fear number will be 2, 1, or 0.

❖ Remember that each step should be planned (decide when you are going to do it) and repeated (do the step over and over until it is not so scary anymore).

If this plan seems scary, remember that you will do it a little at a time, and eventually you will get over your fear!

Sample Picture It Poster
Fear of Dogs

REWARD:
Go for ice cream,
I get 2 scoops!

I CAN DO THIS!

Last Step:
Pet the dog for
five minutes.

7th Step:
Holds the dog's
leash

6th Step:
Stand beside the dog without
touching it; hold parent's hand.

5th Step:
Go to the park and watch dogs; move a
little closer to the dogs.

4th Step:
Go to the park to watch dogs from far away; hold
parent's hand.

3rd Step:
Look at the dog through the window.

2nd Step:
Watch a video with dogs in it.

1st Step:
Look at pictures of dogs.

(Version for younger children)

Sample Tracking Sheet

(Fill this in <u>before</u> you do this step on your Picture It Poster.)

What small step from my Picture It Poster am I about to do?

Look at pictures of dogs.

What's my Finger Fear Rating before I start? (Hold up fingers to show your answer.)

5 fingers = extremely scared   **4 fingers** = a lot scared   **3 fingers** = medium scared
2 fingers = a little scared   **1 finger** = tiny bit scared   **0 fingers** = not scared

3 fingers = medium scared

(Fill this in <u>after</u> you have completed this step on your Picture It Poster.)

Did anything dangerous happen? ___ Yes ✔ No

What's my Finger Fear Rating now? **0 fingers = not scared**

I did it! Hooray for me! Give myself a pat on the back!

(Version for younger children)

Tracking Sheet

(Fill this in <u>before</u> you do this step on your Picture It Poster.)

What small step from my Picture It Poster am I about to do?

What's my Finger Fear Rating before I start? (Hold up fingers to show your answer.)

5 fingers = extremely scared **4 fingers** = a lot scared   **3 fingers** = medium scared
2 fingers = a little scared   **1 finger** = tiny bit scared   **0 fingers** = not scared

(Fill this in <u>after</u> you have completed this step on your Picture It Poster.)

Did anything dangerous happen? ___ Yes ___ No

What's my Finger Fear Rating now? (Hold up fingers to show your answer. Repeat the step until Finger Fear Rating is 2, 1, or 0.)

I did it! Hooray for me! Give myself a pat on the back!

(Version for older children)

Sample Tracking Sheet

(Fill this in <u>before</u> you do this step on your Picture It Poster.)

What small step from my Picture It Poster am I about to do?
Watch YouTube videos of dogs.

What's my Finger Fear Rating before I start? (Hold up fingers to show your answer.)

5 fingers = extremely scared   **4 fingers** = a lot scared   **3 fingers** = medium scared
2 fingers = a little scared   **1 finger** = tiny bit scared   **0 fingers** = not scared

4 fingers = a lot scared

What am I worried will happen?
I'll have a panic attack.

What's the proof this will happen? (How many times has it happened/not happened to me?)
I've had panic attacks before when I was scared.

What are the real chances that this will happen?
Probably won't because I'm taking small steps that I'm ready for, and I know how to cope better now.

How can I handle it if this happens?
Remind myself I can handle this.

(Fill this in <u>after</u> you do this step on your Picture It Poster.)

Was this as bad as I thought it would be? Did I prove I could handle this step?
Not as bad because nothing bad happened. I proved I could handle this!

What's my Finger Fear Rating now? (Hold up fingers to show your answer. Repeat the step until Finger Fear Rating is 2, 1, or 0.)
0 fingers = not scared

I did it! Hooray for me! Give myself a pat on the back!

(Version for older children)

Tracking Sheet

(Fill this in <u>before</u> you do this step on your Picture It Poster.)

What small step from my Picture It Poster am I about to do?

What's my Finger Fear Rating before I start? (Hold up fingers to show your answer.)

5 fingers = extremely scared **4 fingers** = a lot scared   **3 fingers** = medium scared
2 fingers = a little scared   **1 finger** = tiny bit scared   **0 fingers** = not scared

What am I worried will happen?

What's the proof this will happen? (How many times has it happened/not happened to me?)

What are the real chances that this will happen?

How can I handle it if this happens?

(Fill this in <u>after</u> you do this step on your Picture It Poster.)

Was this as bad as I thought it would be? Did I prove I could handle this step?

What's my Finger Fear Rating now? (Hold up fingers to show your answer. Repeat step until Finger Fear Rating is 2, 1, or 0.)

I did it! Hooray for me! Give myself a pat on the back!

Play Clay Role-Play

Facing fears can be hard, so let's do an activity to get you ready. I'm going to pretend that I'm a child who is really afraid of dogs, and we're going to perform a play about facing this fear. Let's make clay figures for the play: We need a child, a parent, and a dog in a window. We'll make simple, quick clay figures so this doesn't take too long.

(The child can decide who makes the child, the parent, and the dog in the window.)

Your parent and I will perform the play while you watch. After we're done, you can tell us if you think we did a good job!

(The parent and practitioner perform the play below. The parent plays the role of parent and the practitioner plays the role of the child. The clay figure of the dog in the window is placed in front of the parent and the practitioner.)

PARENT: Let's go to the pet store and look at dogs in the window.

CHILD: I don't want to. Dogs are scary!

PARENT: What's your Finger Fear Rating?

CHILD: It's 4, because I feel a lot scared.

PARENT: I know that looking at dogs in the window seems scary to you, but you can do this.

CHILD: Okay, I'll try.

PARENT: I'm proud of you for trying!
(Parent and practitioner move their clay figures to show they are looking at the dog in the window.)

CHILD: I looked quickly at the dog in the window. Can we go home now?

PARENT: Let's stick with this for a bit longer until you are able to look at the dog in the window and not feel so scared. What about this seems scary to you?

CHILD: Dogs bite people with their sharp teeth! I don't like dogs.

PARENT: As you're looking at the dog in the window, is anything bad or dangerous happening to you?

CHILD: No.

PARENT: See! You proved that you can look at the dog in the window and nothing bad or dangerous happened to you. How do you feel knowing that nothing bad or dangerous happened to you?

CHILD: A lot better!

PARENT: What's your Finger Fear Rating now?

CHILD: It's 0, because I'm not scared to do this anymore!

PARENT: I'm so proud of you for facing your fear of looking at the dog in the window. Now you're ready to try the next step. Tomorrow we'll go watch the dogs playing at the park.

CHILD: No! That's too scary!

PARENT: Remember, we're going to do this step by step, a little at a time, so it's not so scary. The next step on your Picture It Poster is for us to stand at the entrance to the park, while you hold my hand. Should we do this for five minutes or ten minutes?

CHILD: Five minutes.

PARENT: Okay, that seems like a good next step. I know you are ready to do it.

Now you get to make up your own play about facing your fear. Look at your Picture It Poster to remind yourself of the first step you will do to begin to face your fear. We already made clay figures for you and your parent. Quickly make one or two more clay figures for your play.

For this play, you will hold the clay figure of the child so you can play your part, and your parent will hold the parent clay figure to play the role of parent. Show with the clay figures what you will each do and say to complete the first step on the Picture It Poster.

Recipe for Play Clay

Tape a garbage bag around the work area to contain the mess.

In a medium-sized bowl, mix together:

2 cups of flour
½ cup of salt
2 tablespoons of vegetable oil

Gradually add ½ cup of water to the bowl and mix well. If clay is too dry, add more water a little bit at a time.

Add food coloring to the play clay (you may want to divide the play clay into several clumps first, so you can make different colors).

To keep the play clay soft, place it in a resealable plastic bag.

Best Friend Role-Play

Facing fears can be hard, so let's do an activity to get you ready. Pretend your best friend is afraid to go swimming. Do a role-play about facing this fear. Decide who should play each role. For example, your parent and therapist can each play one of the roles (Friend #1 or Friend #2) while you act as the director of the role-play. Or, you can play one of the roles and your therapist or parent can play the other role. You can change the script if you have ideas to make it better. Write the last part of the script yourself, offering advice to help your best friend cope with this problem. Really imagine what your friend looks like and how they might move and behave.

(Friend #1 and Friend #2 stand facing each other.)

FRIEND #1: It's so hot today! Let's go swimming.

FRIEND #2: I don't want to. I'm not in the mood to go swimming.

FRIEND #1: Oh come on, it'll be fun. Everyone will be at the pool today.

FRIEND #2: Actually, can I tell you a secret?

FRIEND #1: What?

FRIEND #2: Well, it's kind of embarrassing.

FRIEND #1: We're best friends—you can tell me anything.

FRIEND #2: Okay, but promise you won't tell anyone else.

FRIEND #1: K.

FRIEND #2: I'm afraid to go swimming. Like, what if I drown?

FRIEND #1: I know exactly how you feel. I used to be afraid of dogs. But then I went to see a therapist and I got over my fear. Now I'm way happier.

FRIEND #2: How did you get over your fear?

FRIEND #1: We did this thing called an exposure plan. We came up with small steps to help me face my fear a little at a time. I was pretty nervous to do it at first because I worried about all the bad things that could happen. But before I started each step, I said to myself, "I'll be nervous at first, but if I stick with it, I'll realize that it's not bad or dangerous, and then I'll be okay."

114

FRIEND #2: Wow, that seems pretty easy.

FRIEND #1: Actually, it wasn't so easy. There were times when I felt really scared, especially the time when I was holding the dog's leash and it saw another dog across the street and it started to bark and jump. I totally freaked out!

FRIEND #2: What did you do?

FRIEND #1: I ran into my house and I tried to stay away from dogs. But after a few days I realized that I couldn't avoid them forever because lots of people have dogs. Plus, I really wanted to hang out at the park with my friends, and there are a ton of dogs running around at the park. I realized I had to face this fear if I wanted to get rid of it once and for all! So I did the step again, but this time when the dog started to bark I told myself that the dog was just excited, and that it wasn't going to bite me. That helped me keep calm. A few days later I did the last step on my exposure plan—I pet the dog. I did this a few days in a row, until I felt totally comfortable being around dogs.

FRIEND #2: Wow! That's awesome! But I don't think I'm as brave as you.

FRIEND #1: I wasn't so brave at first. But my therapist said, "If you really want to get over your fear, you have to choose to be brave and work at it." I thought this was kind of bossy, but my therapist was right. Now I'm really glad I got over this fear. My life isn't ruled by this fear anymore. I feel a lot happier.

FRIEND #2: I don't want my fear to rule my life either. What do you think I should do?

(Write the last part of this script and act it out together!)

Information Sheet for Parents:
Facing Fears

Key Points

- Your child is learning many strategies to reduce anxiety. Perhaps the most important strategy is facing fears. The process of facing fears is called "exposure." Gradual exposure involves having your child face the feared situation a little at a time until the situation is tolerable.

- Exposure is not dangerous and will not make the fear worse. In fact, your child has probably been avoiding fearful situations, which maintains the anxiety. By engaging in gradual exposure, your child can learn that these situations are not dangerous, and are therefore tolerable.

- We will develop a step-by-step plan to help your child gradually get used to the feared situation so that each step is manageable. Eventually, your child will be able to be in the situation with minimal or no anxiety.

- You play an essential role in helping your child face the feared situation each step of the way, so it is important that you feel comfortable and are in agreement with the plan.

- Following the exposure plan will take time and effort. Doing exposure exercises several times per week has proven more effective than once a week or every couple of weeks. If you have a very busy schedule, let's discuss what you can take off your plate so this can be a priority.

- Your child may resist or refuse to cooperate at various points during the exposure plan. This is normal. Your gut reaction may be to stop the plan. This will not help your child, as it will send the message that the feared situation is insurmountable. We will discuss various strategies to overcome this resistance, including the appropriate use of rewards.

- Once your child has overcome a fear, it is quite common for setbacks to occur. Try not to interpret this as failure. The best way to cope when a fear resurfaces is to recognize that this is normal, to explore possible reasons underlying the setback, and to have a positive and calm approach to brainstorming coping strategies. Sometimes it is helpful to revisit the exposure plan or certain steps of the plan.

Tips

Below are some tips to help you support your child through the exposure plan (adapted from *Freeing Your Child from Anxiety* by Tamar Chansky; *Growing Up Brave* by Donna Pincus; and *Worried No More: Help and Hope for Anxious Children* by Aureen Wagner).

- **DON'T** force your child to face fears or reprimand them for refusing to try.
  DO ask questions to determine what's difficult (e.g., "What are you worried might happen if you do this step?"). Talk with your child about ideas for a smaller step your child can say "yes" to (e.g., "Let's figure out together another step that will move you toward your goal"). Help your child see the benefits of completing the exposure plan (e.g., "How will your life be easier or more fun if you get over this fear?").

- **DON'T** dismiss or ridicule your child's fear.
  DO empathize with your child and encourage success (e.g., Say in a calm, soothing tone, "I know this seems hard to you, but you can do it").

- **DON'T** make all the decisions for your child.
  DO present your child with appropriate options to choose from (e.g., "Do you want to go watch the dogs at the park near our house or at the park next to your school?").

- **DON'T** give extra comfort or attention if your child becomes distressed while doing a step on the fear plan.
  DO make a *brief* statement to reflect and empathize with your child's feelings and encourage continued effort (e.g., Say in a calm, soothing tone, "I understand how hard it is to try this, and I will be very proud of you for trying").

- **DON'T** try to persuade your child out of feeling anxious if your child has a meltdown during the exposure process. Trying to reason with your child in the midst of a meltdown is unhelpful because your child is overly distraught and cannot think clearly.
  DO say in a calm voice, "I will talk with you when you are calm." Let the tantrum run its course. Attend and give praise once your child is calm (e.g., "I really like how you calmed yourself"). Then refocus your child onto the step that is being worked on. (Additional guidance on handling meltdowns can be found in *Worried No More: Help and Hope for Anxious Children*, by Aureen Wagner.)

- **DON'T** give in to your child's pleas to stop in the midst of the exposure plan.
  DO encourage continued effort (e.g., Say in a calm, soothing tone, "I can see that you're scared of the dog because you're clinging to my leg, but you are ready to hold onto the dog's leash"). Remember that your child needs to experience some anxiety in order to overcome it.

- **DON'T** encourage your child to use a relaxation strategy in the midst of the exposure plan as this can interfere with the process.
  DO give a reminder that your child needs to feel the fear in order to overcome it.

- **DON'T** try to distract your child during an exposure exercise.
  DO help your child be emotionally engaged while doing the steps on the exposure plan. This means facing and feeling what is happening in the present moment, rather than avoiding the feared situation. During an exposure exercise, if you notice that your child is avoiding the feared situation, ask your child: "What feels scary to you right now?" or "What do you see or hear that is scaring you?" Keep any questions brief and focused on the feared situation.

- **DON'T** rush a step or stop it too soon. Your child needs to stick with it for a certain amount of time so they learn that the bad things they fear won't happen and the situation is tolerable. If you end an exposure practice when your child's anxiety is still high, it leaves your child with the memory that this step is scary. Your child may then be reluctant to continue exposure exercises.
  DO reassure your child that staying in the scary situation eventually makes it become less scary. Remind your child that the goal is to stay in the scary situation (or repeat the step) until the fear level goes down from maybe "a lot" to "a little" (e.g., Say in a calm, soothing tone, "I can see that this is uncomfortable for you. Stick with it and you will soon realize that nothing bad or dangerous is happening to you. This will make the really scared feelings go away").

- **DO** praise your child after the step on the exposure plan is completed (e.g., "I'm so proud of you for holding the dog's leash"). Also encourage your child to self-praise (e.g., "What good feelings do you have about yourself after completing this step?").

- **DON'T** totally stop facing the fear even once your child has overcome it.
  DO provide opportunities in the future for your child to be in the original feared situation. This is called "relapse prevention." For example, if your child overcame a fear of dogs, provide ongoing opportunities for your child to pet dogs.

Section 8

Parenting Skills

Cognitive behavioral therapy includes regular sessions with the child's parents. The focus of these sessions includes enhancing parents' feelings of efficacy, increasing parents' understanding and practicing of skills related to the treatment components, and teaching parenting skills. The activities in this section present creative ideas for parents to utilize with their anxious child, as well as with their other children.

Learning new ways to approach parenting takes courage and motivation, and parents should be praised for their efforts to change. Parents who feel particularly challenged by their child's behavior may benefit from a more intensive parenting program. Parents who are highly anxious or who have other significant mental health problems will benefit from a referral to their own individual treatment.

Interventions

Brag Book (Child Version) (page 122)
Ages: 5–12
Objective: Parent to appropriately praise child's positive behavior; increase child's positive view of self
Supplies: Small notebook, pen
Description:
The Brag Book is a concrete tool to help parents praise their child daily. Labeled praise is best taught through a combination of verbal discussion and role-plays in parent sessions, followed by coaching in conjoint sessions. The Brag Book should be introduced to parents early in the intervention process as it facilitates a positive parent–child relationship and optimizes the child's outcome. Parents can bring the Brag Book to sessions and read aloud a few excerpts. This provides the child with additional positive attention. In-session modeling and practicing of labeled praise will help illustrate and reinforce the technique. An efficacious method of modeling the use of the Brag Book is for the practitioner to have a small notebook for the client, and to write in it a few labeled praise statements at the end of each session. The labeled praise statement can highlight a skill learned that session, or some other therapeutic gain made by the child and parent. For example, the practitioner can say to the child, "You listened really carefully today as I was teaching you the Cookie Breathing technique, and now you know how to use it to calm your body. Way to go!" A praise for the parent could be: "I really liked how you let your child take the lead today when we were coming up with ideas for the exposure plan."

Brag Book (Parent Version) (page 123)
Ages: N/A
Objective: Increase positive parenting practices
Supplies: Small notebook, pen
Description:
Children make greater progress when their parents encourage and promote non-anxious behavior. Parents can model relaxation skills, affective expression, cognitive coping, and facing anxiety-provoking situations. The parent version of the Brag Book is a tool to increase and document the parents' use of modeling and positive parenting practices. It also helps parents to self-praise.

Table Talk (page 124)
Ages: 6–16
Objective: Increase open communication between parent and child
Description:
Open communication is the basis for positive parent–child relationships. It involves not only what children verbalize to their parents but also the parents' ability to actively listen to their child. The parents are encouraged to implement Table Talk on a daily basis and to use reflective listening skills. Reflective listening validates the child's experience and communicates empathy and understanding. It also encourages deeper communication. Table Talk is encouraged during dinnertime rather than at bedtime, as anxious children may have difficulty settling for sleep if conversations happen right before bed. Communication skills are best taught through a combination of verbal discussion and role-plays in parent sessions, followed by coaching in conjoint sessions.

Reward Bag (page 125)
Ages: 6–12
Objective: Increase child's positive behavior
Supplies: Gift bag, scissors
Description:
The appropriate use of rewards will help motivate the child to practice skills learned in therapy and to progress on the fear ladder. The Reward Bag is created with the parent and child together. The child is given appropriate choices for the reward items to encourage interest and motivation. Reward items are suggested that facilitate fun parent–child interaction.

Play Date (page 127)
Ages: 6–12
Objective: Increase pleasurable time spent between parent and child
Description:
Children need quality time with their parents. The Play Date is a simple way to facilitate this. If the relationship between a parent and child is strained, the parent will need additional guidance from the practitioner on how to engage the child, plan the activities for the play date, preempt potential problems, and debrief after the play date. Activities that are overly expensive, competitive, or that have minimal parent–child interaction should be discouraged. The Play Date is an intervention to help strengthen the positive connection between parent and child; therefore, the planned play date should not be viewed as a reward for good behavior, nor should it be cancelled for misbehavior.

Success Story (page 128)

Ages: 6–16

Objective: Verbalize an ability to manage challenging situations

Description:

Anxious children are filled with self-doubt regarding their ability to face difficult circumstances. Reminding them of past successes and achievements can help them realize they have the potential to manage future challenges. Sharing stories with children about times they achieved a difficult task can connect them back to their successes and remind them that they are capable (Wilson & Lyons, 2013). Parents might need guidance to create their stories or scrapbooks to ensure the content captures the essence of proud moments. Thus, this intervention can be initiated in a session between practitioner and parent, continued in a parent–child session, and completed by parent and child at home.

Brag Book (Child Version)

Children with anxiety struggle with low self-esteem. They lack confidence in their abilities to manage daily situations and they often feel that others are disappointed with them. The Brag Book will help you elevate your child's self-esteem and will also encourage better behavior. Here's how to do it:

- Get a notebook and label/decorate the cover (e.g., Brag Book: Jamie's Awesome, Incredible, Amazing Good Behavior). Keep the book by your child's bed.

- Catch your child being good (aim for at least four times per day) and focus on this good behavior by using labeled praise. This means telling your child exactly what they are doing that you like. It is especially helpful to praise your child's efforts, use of new coping skills, and appropriate behaviors. Below are some examples of labeled praise:

- *I appreciate the effort you put into (cleaning your room).*

- *I like that you (listened when I asked you to brush your teeth).*

- *I'm proud of you for (going to the party even though you felt nervous).*

- *(You did deep breathing to calm yourself when you felt anxious.) Way to go!*

- Each night at bedtime, write in the book one positive thing that your child did that day, then read the "brag" statement to your child.

- Since praise is most effective when given immediately after the positive behavior occurs, try to use labeled praise at the appropriate time during the day, then reinforce the praise statement at night when you do the Brag Book (e.g., *Thanks for listening when I asked you to put your toys away. Tonight I'm going to write in your Brag Book about how proud I am that you showed good listening!*).

- Do not add a negative statement after you have praised your child. For example, do not say, *Thanks for listening when I asked you to put your toys away. Why can't you listen like that more often?* This phrasing turns your positive statement into a negative criticism of your child.

- Focus on the effort not the outcome. This means recognizing when your child has tried hard. For example, if your child is not the best soccer player but tries hard, you should praise this effort.

If you praise your child often and do the Brag Book each night, you will soon notice a positive change in your child's behavior. This will lead to a more positive environment at home and elevate your child's self-esteem!

Brag Book (Parent Version)

You play a crucial role in reducing your child's anxiety. Modeling (showing) calm, healthy coping and responding to your child in helpful ways can improve and maintain your child's progress. The Brag Book (Parent Version) can help you keep track of ways you are modeling healthy coping and responding to your child in helpful ways. Here's how to do it:

Get a small notebook and label it Brag Book (Parent Version). Each day (or at least a few times a week), write down what you are doing to model or show calm, healthy coping, and helpful ways in which you are responding to your child. It's okay to "brag" or give yourself credit for your efforts! Below are examples:

- Used diaphragmatic breathing to calm my body and encouraged my child to do the same.

- Replaced unhelpful thoughts with helpful thoughts and encouraged my child to do the same.

- Encouraged my child using empathy: "I know this is hard for you, but you can do it!"

- Praised my child's effort or ability to face a feared situation.

- Labeled my emotions to help my child understand feelings.

- Listened to and validated my child's feelings.

- Coached my child to complete the Practice at Home exercise.

Below is an example of a Brag Book entry:

Date: April 14
Situation: Got a cavity filled at the dentist
What I did and/or said to help my child:
Said to my child, "I was nervous to get a cavity filled at the dentist because I knew it was going to hurt. But I reminded myself that I have gotten through painful dental procedures before and I'll get through this one too. And I did Cookie Breathing to help myself get calm."

Keep the Brag Book by your bed. Try to write in it each day. It will help you keep track of ways you are helping your child to succeed. And it will remind you of the great job you are doing as a parent!

Table Talk

Provide regular opportunities for your children to talk with you. Table Talk is one strategy you can use. Try to incorporate Table Talk into your dinner routine: Ask each child, "How was your day today? Was it a happy day or a sad day? What happened to make it a happy day or a sad day?" (For older children ask, "How was your day today on a scale of one to ten, one being the worst possible day and ten being the best day ever?") Listening to your children and responding in a supportive manner will invite more open communication. Here are some tips:

- Maintain eye contact and nod to show you are focused and attentive.

- Listen carefully, focus on your child's feelings, and avoid talking about your own feelings.

- Summarize what you heard (e.g., "You felt sad when…").

- Validate your child's feelings using a soft tone of voice (e.g., "You must have felt sad when the other kids wouldn't let you play with them").

- Ask open-ended questions to invite more discussion (e.g., "Tell me more about your sad feelings").

Don't feel like you have to make it all better—simply listening to your children and validating their feelings is what your children need most from you.

During Table Talk, your child might bring up situations that are causing anxiety. Respond by validating feelings rather than agreeing with or negating fears. Here is an example:

CHILD: I had a sad day because you were late picking me up and I was worried that you got into a car accident.
UNHELPFUL RESPONSE: It was silly of you to worry about that.
HELPFUL RESPONSE: Today was a sad day because you had a big worry. Tell me more about your feelings.

Try your very best to do Table Talk every day. If you and your child won't be together at dinner, find other times in the day to talk. For example, you can have Car Talk while driving your child home from school or to an activity.

Reward Bag

A reward system is a helpful way to encourage your child's positive behavior. Create a Reward Bag with your child. Reward items can include fun parent–child activities and special treats. Decide together on the rewards so your child feels part of the process and is motivated to earn the rewards (see suggestions below). Write each reward item on a separate slip of paper, fold it, and place it in the bag.

Ideas for the Reward Bag

Play a board game with parent

Build a fort with parent

Play dress-up with parent

Do a craft with parent

Find a new recipe together, then make it

Build something out of Lego with parent

Work on a puzzle together

Make chocolate fondue together

Have a family indoor picnic

Have breakfast in bed

Take a bubble bath

Get 30 minutes extra TV/computer time

Make a playlist of top ten favorite songs

Have a "reverse dinner" (eat dessert first)

Go for ice cream

Your child can earn a point each time the target behavior is accomplished. Points can be traded in for a small reward (e.g., 5 points = 1 reward). Track points earned by using a reward chart (see sample chart below). Keep the chart in a convenient and visible place so everyone remembers.

Target behavior	1	2	3	4	5	Reward I will get
Practice Cookie Breathing						Bubble bath

Below are some guidelines to help make the reward system effective:

Be selective: Choose only one target behavior to reward at a time. Begin by selecting a target behavior that is easy to do, as this will create positive energy and motivation. The target behavior may relate to anxiety issues (e.g., practice Cookie Breathing before bedtime) or general compliance (e.g., listen the first time when asked to do something). Gradually fade out rewards for success with a target behavior as the task gets easier, then switch the reward to another target behavior.

Be clear: Explain to your child exactly what needs to be done to earn a point and how many points are needed to pick a reward from the bag (e.g., "You get 1 point each time you practice Cookie Breathing before bed. Each time you earn 5 points, you get to pick something from the prize bag"). When your child earns a reward, give extra positive reinforcement by verbally stating to your child what the reward is for (e.g., "You're getting to play a board game with me tonight because you practiced Cookie Breathing before bed for five days. I'm so proud of you for learning to calm your body"). Do not create a reward system that requires your child to do a task for a certain number of days in a row, as this is too much pressure. For example, instead of "You get to pick a reward from the bag when you sleep in your own bed five days in a row," make it "You get to pick a reward from the bag when you sleep in your own bed for five nights."

Be consistent: Give a point every time your child earns one. If you only give points when you remember or when it's convenient, your child will become frustrated and unmotivated.

Be immediate: Give the point as soon as it is earned and let your child pick a reward from the bag as soon as sufficient points have been earned. If you are not able to give the reward immediately, be sure to work it into your schedule and let your child know when the reward will be received (e.g., "You worked so hard to earn this ice cream. Tomorrow after school will be our special time for you to get this treat!")

Be positive: If your child does not engage in the target behavior, the point is not awarded. However, rather than dwelling on this, be positive by letting your child know when there will be another opportunity to earn a point. Never take away a point or a reward once it has been earned, and do not give a punishment if a goal is not achieved.

Play Date

Your child needs regular quality time with you. Having regular "play dates" with your child will encourage this time together and strengthen your bond with your child. This special time has three parts: planning, doing, and evaluating.

Planning

Decide with your child what you will do together for your play date, and when you will do it. It need not be an expensive outing. Doing a craft, building a fort, or baking cookies are great ways to spend quality time together. You and your child can each suggest a few ideas for your play date, then let your child choose something from the list. It is best if it is something fun and interactive. Avoid activities that are competitive or that have little interaction, like playing computer games or going to a movie. Also avoid going somewhere that will detract from one-on-one time with your child, like a park. Plan the date and time and mark it on your calendar. If you have to cancel, be sure to reschedule to avoid disappointing your child.

Doing

Maintain a positive interaction during this special time with your child. This is not the time for criticizing or punishing. Only set limits if your child is doing something hurtful, otherwise, let it go! If your child becomes overly anxious, model appropriate coping. The activity you do is less important than the interaction, so be relaxed and playful, focus on your child's positive behavior, and give your child your undivided attention.

Evaluating

Talk with your child afterward about the time spent together. If you'd like, you can use the evaluation below:

Evaluation of Our Play Date

What we did together: _____

Child's rating: I had a (circle one) bad/good/great time because:

Parent's rating: I had a (circle one) bad/good/great time because:

Plan a play date regularly with your child. Aim for at least 30 minutes once a week.

Success Story

Children enjoy hearing positive stories about themselves. Telling stories to your child that recount their personal achievements will elevate their self-esteem and build their confidence to face challenges. Write a story then read it to your child. (If this is too time-consuming, jot down a few key points then elaborate during storytelling time.) Focus your story on times when your child learned a new skill, faced a fear, or overcame a challenge. If your child was highly anxious during the scenario, highlight how your child made it through and survived the feared situation. Below are some story theme ideas:

- Learned to walk

- Learned to ride a bike

- First day of school

- Went to the dentist for the first time

- Performed in the school play

Don't be afraid to touch on funny moments, provided that they will not embarrass your child. Use esteem-building language and phrases that highlight your child's efforts and perseverance, such as:

- *You didn't know how but you tried and tried and eventually you did it.*

- *You were scared but you did it anyway.*

- *You learned that you could make it through tough times.*

- *You faced this challenge and you did it.*

End your story with a positive message that conveys how proud you were of your child.

The story does not need to be long but should include descriptive detail. When you tell your story, be animated and maintain eye contact with your child. Create a nurturing environment, such as rubbing your child's back as you tell the story.

As an alternative to writing a story, you could prepare a scrapbook or keepsake box with photos and mementos and add captions that highlight how your child succeeded at each task. This can be a helpful starting point for sharing stories with your child about past successes.

Section 9

Termination

The final phase of treatment allows a unique opportunity for the practitioner to provide the client with a positive goodbye experience—one that the client is appropriately prepared for and one that is embedded with positive messages. The goals are to review and celebrate the successes and accomplishments made, reflect on the client's new abilities to cope more effectively, and provide a healthy model for saying goodbye.

It is best practice to raise the topic of termination with clients well in advance of the final sessions. In fact, graduating from therapy can be discussed at the outset of treatment so clients can understand that there is a beginning, a middle, and an end to therapy, and can then look forward to the final celebration. As well, the child can be reminded about the end of treatment at various points throughout therapy (e.g., "You've worked hard and accomplished these five goals in therapy. Let's talk about the goals we will work on in the remaining six sessions").

Relapse prevention is a key focus in the final sessions of therapy. An important goal is to prepare children and their parents to expect anxiety from time to time, and to emphasize that continued practice and use of skills learned in therapy can assist in dealing with setbacks. Relapse prevention also entails presenting children with challenging scenarios that they might encounter in the future and helping them to problem-solve appropriate ways of managing potential fears or worries.

A letter can be written to give to the child at the last session (see sample Letter from the Therapist in Appendix E). The letter can be modified so it is tailored to the client, reviews specific goals achieved in therapy, and provides healing messages.

The child is given the scrapbook to take home at the last session. It is important to discuss with the parents where in the child's home the scrapbook will be kept to ensure its privacy and safekeeping. Time can be devoted in the last session to reviewing parts of the scrapbook. (Note: it is important to abide by professional policies and procedures regarding the storage of files, and, if mandated, a copy of the child's scrapbook should be made for the file before giving it to the child.)

The scrapbook becomes a transitional object for the client, as it is a permanent connection to therapy. Moreover, the healing messages from the practitioner's letter provide a reminder that the client is cared for, which strengthens feelings of self-worth.

Parent's participation in the child's last session can enhance the termination process. However, it is important to meet with the parents in advance of the last session to enlist their involvement and to prepare them. The practitioner can coach the parents to write their own letter to their child, to be read in the last session (see Guidelines for Letter from the Parents in Appendix F).

Interventions

Cookie Jar (page 132)
Ages: 6–10
Objective: Articulate why, when, and how therapy will end
Supplies: Plastic jar or container with lid, adhesive label, marker, five cookies
Advance Preparation:
Place five cookies in a jar, stick the label on the outside of the jar, and label it with the child's name (e.g., Jamie's Cookie Jar).
Description:
Children often lack the cognitive ability to fully understand a concept such as the termination of therapy. Cookie Jar provides a visual and concrete way to help young clients understand when and how therapy will end. The activity helps to prepare clients for termination and reduces anxiety and feelings of abandonment. This intervention should be used in conjunction with other termination activities that help celebrate the client's therapeutic achievements and that facilitate the goodbye process. It is best to introduce this activity once there are five sessions left. Clear limits must be set regarding the cookies, as children may be tempted to eat them all at once!

Balloon Bash (page 133)
Ages: 6–8
Objective: Review and articulate concepts learned in therapy
Supplies: Balloons, timer
Advance Preparation:
Blow up a balloon and knot it.
Description:
Balloon Bash helps children review and evaluate their experiences in therapy. The balloon is symbolic of the celebratory nature of this termination activity and is given to clients at the end as a parting gift. It is a good idea to have extra balloons on hand in case one pops during the activity.

Crumpled Paper Throw: The Sequel (page 134)
Ages: 8–12
Objective: Review and articulate concepts learned in therapy
Supplies: Paper, bag filled with small prizes
Description:
The original version of Crumpled Paper Throw in Section Three: Psychoeducation focused on teaching children about anxiety, symptoms, and treatment. The goal of this second version is to consolidate skills learned, review therapeutic achievements, and prepare children for possible relapse.

Coping with Anxiety Envelope Game (page 135)

Ages: 8–12

Objective: Identify the need for continued use of cognitive behavioral therapy skills

Supplies: Four small envelopes, scissors, dice, bag filled with small prizes

Advance Preparation:

Cut out the four game cards (see page 136), fold them, place each one in a separate envelope, and seal the envelopes.

Description:

This intervention promotes problem-solving and relapse prevention. The game prepares children to expect anxiety from time to time, and emphasizes that continued practice and use of CBT skills can assist in dealing with setbacks. Though some modification of the scenarios may be appropriate, they need not match the child's exact circumstances, as children benefit from problem-solving a variety of anxiety-related issues.

Cookie Jar

You have worked hard in therapy and you have learned so much! This means you are almost ready to stop coming to therapy. This activity is called Cookie Jar. It will help you understand when and how therapy will end so you will feel ready.

Open the cookie jar, take out one cookie (only one!), and eat the cookie. The remaining cookies in the jar show how many more times you will be coming here. There are four cookies left in the jar. So you will be coming here four more times, and then you and I will be saying goodbye to each other. Place the lid on the cookie jar.

Ask me to say something you have learned or accomplished in therapy and to tell you why you are almost ready to stop coming to therapy.

We'll repeat this activity at the end of our next three sessions (e.g., eat one cookie from the cookie jar, count the remaining cookies in the jar, and say how many more times you will be coming to therapy). At the end of the three sessions, there will be one cookie left in the cookie jar, which means you will come to therapy one last time. The last time you come will be special. It will be a celebration of all you have accomplished in therapy. It will be a time for us to say a last goodbye to each other.

At the end of your last session, you will get to eat the last cookie left in the jar.

Balloon Bash

You have worked hard in therapy and you have learned so much! Balloon Bash will help you talk about some of the things you did in therapy. To play, throw the balloon up in the air and try to keep it in the air for 30 seconds without it touching the ground. When 30 seconds is up (or when the balloon touches the ground), answer one of the questions below. Repeat until all the questions have been answered. At the end, you can take home the balloon as a celebration of all your hard work in therapy!

1. You learned that when you are scared or worried, your body feels different. What is one thing that happens in your body when you feel scared or worried?

2. You learned ways to relax your body. Pretend you are feeling scared or worried, and show what you can do to relax your body.

3. You got better at talking about upset feelings. Tell about a time when you felt sad, angry, or worried.

4. You learned that thinking calm, helpful thoughts makes you feel better. Which one is a calm, helpful thought that can help you feel better?

    This is too scary; I can't do this.
    OR
    I'll be fine; I can do this.

5. You learned to face your fear. What is something that used to make you feel really worried or scared that you are able to do now without feeling so worried or scared?

6. We did lots of activities together in therapy. Which activity did you like best?

Crumpled Paper Throw: The Sequel

This version of Crumpled Paper Throw will help you talk about the important things you learned in therapy. To play, crumple a piece of paper into a ball, stand behind the tape line, and throw the paper ball toward the hoop I make with my arms. If you get the crumpled paper through the hoop, you earn 1 point. If you miss, I'll ask you a question. You get 2 points for each question you answer. At the end of the game, trade in points for prizes: 1–10 points = 1 prize; 11 or more points = 2 prizes.

You learned that when you are anxious or worried, your body feels different. What are some of the changes that happen in your body when you are anxious?

You learned ways to express upset feelings. Tell about a time recently when you felt sad, angry, jealous, embarrassed, or worried.

Take a break to move your body: Show with your face and body what proud looks like.

You learned that unhelpful thoughts make you feel more anxious, and helpful thoughts can make you feel better. Give an example of an unhelpful thought that can make you feel anxious or worried, then replace this unhelpful thought with a helpful thought.

You learned that facing your fears can make the really scared feelings go away. Pretend you are offering advice to another kid who has big fears, and explain how facing these fears can make the really scared feelings go away.

You made great progress on overcoming your big fears. But it's normal for worries and fears to pop up again. When this happens, what can you do to cope with your fear and make the really scared feelings go away?

Take a break to move your body: Show with your body what you can do to get calm when you feel scared or worried.

You did many activities in therapy. Which activity was your favorite?

Children have different feelings about ending therapy. Some children feel happy to end therapy; some children feel upset about ending therapy. How do you feel about ending therapy?

You worked hard in therapy and had many proud moments. What are you most proud of?

Take a break to move your body: Give yourself a pat on the back to show what a great job you did in therapy.

Coping with Anxiety Envelope Game

You learned a lot in therapy about ways to cope with problems and worries. This game will help you review what you learned. To play the game, roll the dice. If you roll an odd number (1, 3, 5) you get 1 point. If you roll an even number (2, 4, 6) pick an envelope, open it, and answer the question. You get 2 points for each question you answer correctly. At the end of the game, trade in points for prizes: 1–10 points = 1 prize; 11 or more points = 2 prizes.

Coping with Anxiety Envelope Game
Question Cards

It's the first day back at school after summer break and you're feeling scared and nervous. Circle the best way to cope with this:

(a) You should think to yourself, "I'm going to have a panic attack!"
(b) You should hide under your bed and refuse to go to school.
(c) You should think to yourself, "I've learned ways to cope with fears. I can handle this."

You worked hard in therapy to overcome your fear of bees. You're outside playing and you get stung by a bee. Now you're afraid to go outside. Circle the best way to cope with this:

(a) You should think to yourself, "Therapy was a total failure!"
(b) You should do some of the steps on your Picture It Poster to gradually face this fear again and get yourself back on track.
(c) You should never go outside again.

You wake up from a nightmare and feel panicked. Circle the best way to cope with this:

(a) You should think to yourself, "I can't handle this!"
(b) You should run to your parent's bedroom crying.
(c) You should do deep breathing until you feel calm. You should also regularly practice the relaxation strategies learned in therapy so you remember them and can use them when you need to calm your anxiety.

You feel anxious about ending therapy, as you're not sure you'll be able to cope with fears and worries that come up in the future. Circle the best way to cope with this:

(a) You should remind yourself that you're ending therapy because you've learned effective ways of coping with fears and worries.
(b) You should yell at your therapist and demand to continue coming to therapy.
(c) You should tell your parent(s) to take you to another therapist.

Information Sheet for Parents:
Termination

Key Points

- The last phase of your child's therapy is a time to review goals achieved, process feelings about ending treatment, and prepare for a positive termination from therapy. We will work together to help make your child's last session a special and celebratory experience.

- Children may be anxious about ending therapy. This can result in a crisis. So don't be alarmed if your child deteriorates toward the end of therapy. This can usually be addressed by empowering your child to use the coping skills learned in therapy.

Tips

- Your child will be given the scrapbook to take home in the last session. Keep the scrapbook in a safe, private place. Encourage your child to look through the scrapbook every so often as a way to reinforce concepts learned in therapy.

- Continue to utilize the parenting skills and coping techniques learned in therapy, like labeled praise, Table Talk, relaxation strategies, and thinking helpful thoughts. This will maintain the positive changes you and your family have made.

- Provide regular opportunities for your child to practice facing feared situations. This is called "relapse prevention." For example, if your child overcame a fear of dogs, provide ongoing opportunities for your child to pet dogs.

- If your child has minor setbacks, offer a reminder to use healthy coping skills and provide additional emotional support. It may also be helpful to schedule periodic therapy "check-up" sessions in the future to provide your child with ongoing support and intervention. Returning briefly to therapy does not signal a failure or the need to start all over again. Sometimes it can simply be helpful to reinforce coping skills and to develop a mini fear plan to get your child back on track.

Appendix A

Teacher Questionnaire

Source: *Creative CBT Interventions for Children with Anxiety*, Liana Lowenstein, 2016

Date: _____ Child's Name: _____ Grade: _____

Name of School: _____ Name of Teacher: _____

Teacher's Phone #: _____ Teacher's Email: _____

How long have you known the child?

_____

_____

Describe the child's academic performance (e.g., below/above average, poor attention, motivated):

_____

_____

_____

Describe the child's behavioral presentation (e.g., well-behaved, disruptive, noncompliant, aggressive, withdrawn):

_____

_____

_____

Describe the child's emotional presentation (e.g., well-adjusted, happy, sad, angry, anxious):

_____

_____

_____

Describe the child's peer relationships (e.g., makes friends easily, few or no friends, bullies, bullied, excessively shy):

_____

_____

Describe any fears or anxieties the child may have:

_____

_____

How does the child deal with anxiety (e.g., cries, yells, leaves class, asks to call home)?

_____

_____

_____

How do you respond to the child's anxiety? Have any accommodations been made at school?

_____

_____

_____

Describe an incident in which the child displayed excessive anxiety, and how it was handled:

_____

_____

_____

Have you met the child's parent(s), and if so, what are your impressions?

_____

_____

_____

_____

How would you rate your knowledge of anxiety symptoms and disorders (excellent, good, fair, poor)?

_____

_____

Please add any other information about the child and family that you feel is important:

_____

_____

_____

_____

_____

_____

_____

_____

Appendix B

Supporting Anxious Students: Tips for School Personnel

Source: *Creative CBT Interventions for Children with Anxiety*, Liana Lowenstein, 2016

Anxiety disorders are among the most common mental health problems of childhood. There are ways you can help anxious children in the school setting. Below are some general tips:

- Talk with students about situations at school that trigger anxiety, and discuss stress-reducing strategies they would find helpful.

- Collaborate with the child's parent(s) and therapist to ensure skills learned in therapy sessions are generalized to the school setting.

- Be consistent with the child's parent(s) and with other school personnel in understanding and handling the child's anxiety.

- Use the same vocabulary for anxiety-related terms that are used by the child's parent(s) and therapist.

- Do not belittle the child's fears and worries. They may appear unwarranted or unrealistic but they feel real to the child.

- Remain calm and relaxed; provide a comforting presence.

- Try not to put the child "on the spot" or draw attention to their anxiety.

- Praise the child's efforts when you notice they have successfully used anxiety-reducing strategies.

- If anxiety is getting in the way of timely completion of homework, provide time estimates for each assignment so the child can attempt to stay within the estimated time.

- Coach the child to use relaxation techniques. Rather than singling out the anxious child, incorporate these strategies into your classroom routine. This will help everyone in the class maintain a sense of calm and focus.

- Incorporate books into the reading curriculum that address children with anxiety. This benefits the child with anxiety and helps other students empathize with children who suffer from this condition.

- Create learning opportunities for your whole class on ways to cope with common stressful situations such as test anxiety, bullying, substitute teachers, etc. Role-plays and other creative, experiential learning methods usually work best.

- Children who refuse to go to school because of anxiety, or who have a social anxiety disorder or selective mutism, require a more specialized plan. Discuss with the child's parent(s) and therapist ways you can support this plan.

141

Schools often put into place accommodations for anxious children, such as permitting the child to call home when feeling highly anxious, allowing the child to present an oral report to the teacher alone rather than to the whole class, and extending time on tests. These accommodations maintain the child's anxiety in the long-term. While accommodations may be helpful initially, there should be an appropriate weaning-off plan. This involves gradually helping the child to face anxiety-provoking situations, and coaching them to apply anxiety-reducing coping strategies.

Educating yourself about anxiety will help you better support anxious students. The Internet is a great source of free resources and articles. There are also many books on the topic. Below are a few recommended resources:

Websites

Anxiety and Depression Association of America: www.adaa.org

AnxietyBC: www.anxietybc.com

National Institute of Mental Health: www.nimh.nih.org

Worry Wise Kids: www.worrywisekids.org

Resources

Worried No More: Help and Hope for Anxious Children by A. Wagner (2005)

Anxiety and OCD at School (CD Rom) by A. Wagner (2012)

Anxiety and Depression in the Classroom: A Teacher's Guide to Fostering Self-Regulation in Young Students by N. Reilly (2015)

Appendix C

Points Tracking Sheet

Put a checkmark when you earn 1 point. Get a prize each time you earn 10 points!

1	2	3	4	5	6	7	8	9	10	Prize
										☺
										☺
										☺
										☺
										☺
										☺
										☺
										☺
										☺
										☺
										☺
										☺
										☺
										☺
										☺
										☺
										☺
										☺
										☺
										☺
										☺
										☺
										☺
										☺
										☺
										☺
										☺
										☺
										☺
										☺
										☺
										☺
										☺
										☺
										☺
										☺

Appendix D

To be completed by client midway through treatment

Therapy Feedback Form

**I value your honest feedback regarding your experience with me.
Please take a few moments to complete this form.**

Date: _____ Name: _____

What have you found most helpful about therapy?

_____

_____

_____

_____

What are you and your child able to do better now?

_____

_____

_____

_____

Is there anything that could make your therapeutic experience better?

_____

_____

_____

_____

Other comments:

_____

_____

_____

_____

_____

Thanks for your feedback!

Appendix E

Sample Graduation Letter

March 8, 2016

Dear Jamie,

Congratulations on your graduation from therapy! You have worked very hard, and you can feel proud of all that you have accomplished.

When you first came to see me, you had a lot of worries and fears. We did many activities to help you talk about your feelings, understand about worry and anxiety, and learn ways to feel better. You especially enjoyed Crumpled Paper Throw and the Guess Which Hand games. You became an expert at Cookie Breathing and now you know how to calm your body when you feel anxious. You learned so much — hooray for you!

It took a lot of courage to face your fears. You did it a little at a time, step by step, and you were so proud of yourself when you accomplished your goals. When you are faced with worries and fears in the future, you will know the strategies that can help you cope.

Jamie, I want to tell you how lucky I feel to have known you. You are a truly amazing kid! I wish you lots of smiley faces in your bright and exciting future!

Yours truly,

Liana Lowenstein

Appendix F

Guidelines for Letter from the Parents
(for the child's last session)

The last session is an opportunity to highlight and celebrate your child's progress in therapy. You can help make this last session special by writing a letter to your child that you will read in the last session. The letter will then be placed in your child's scrapbook. Here are some suggestions of what to include in the letter. These are just guidelines—feel free to change the wording and include other things that will be meaningful to your child.

- **Comment on the progress your child has made in therapy. Be as specific as possible;** for example, *When you started therapy, you had a tough time dealing with your worries. Now you know different strategies for handling worries. I am proud of you and all the new things you learned to do!*

- **Boost your child's self-esteem:** Parents play an important role in helping their children feel good about themselves. You can raise your child's self-esteem by including in your letter some specific things that are special about your child; for example, *You have so many wonderful qualities. I feel so lucky to have such a kind, thoughtful, amazing kid like you!*

- **End with a loving message:** Although you probably tell your child over and over that you love them, it is still important to include a loving message at the end of your letter. Write whatever comes from your heart!

Please bring two copies of the letter to the session—we will put one in your child's scrapbook, and one in the file.

Appendix G

Books and Resources for Children

Don't Feed the Worry Bug (book and plush) by A. Green

The Hyena Who Lost Her Laugh by J. Lamb-Shapiro

I Can Relax (CD) by D. Pincus

Indigo Dreams (CD) by L. Lite

Master of Mindfulness: How to Be Your Own Superhero in Times of Stress by L. Grossman & A. Alvarez

Moonbeam: *A Book of Meditations for Children by M. Garth*

My Medication Workbook by G. Yorke

The Opposite by T. MacRae & E. Odriozola

Playing with Anxiety: Casey's Guide for Teens and Kids by R. Wilson & L. Lyons

Please Explain Anxiety to Me by L. & J. Zelinger

Sam's Big Secret: Coping with Fear by S. Margolese

Sitting Still Like a Frog: Mindfulness Exercises for Kids by E. Snel

Thinking About Thoughts by L. Matlow

Up and Down the Worry Hill: A Children's Book about OCD and Its Treatment by A. Pinto Wagner

Wanda's Monster by E. Spinelli

What to Do When Mistakes Make You Quake: A Kids Guide to Accepting Imperfection by C. Freeland & J. Toner

What to Do When You Dread Your Bed: A Kid's Guide to Overcoming Problems with Sleep by D. Huebner

Wilma Jean and the Worry Machine by J. Cook

Yoga Pretzels: 50 Fun Yoga Activities for Kids and Grownups: T. Guber & L. Kalish

References and Suggested Reading

Beidel, D.C., & Turner, S.M. (2006). *Shy children, phobic adults* (2nd ed.). Washington, DC: American Psychological Association.

Berman, S.L., Weems, C.F., Silverman, W.K., & Kurtines, W.M. (2000). Predictors of outcome in exposure-based cognitive and behavioral treatments for phobic and anxiety disorders in children. *Behavior Therapy*, 31:713–731.

Cavett, A. (2010). *Structured play-based interventions for engaging children and adolescents in therapy*. West Conshohocken, PA: Infinity Publishing.

Choudhury, M.S., Pimental, S.S., Kendall, P.C. (2003). Childhood anxiety disorders: Parent-child (dis)agreement using a structured interview for the DSM-IV. *Journal of the American Academy for Child and Adolescent Psychiatry*, 42:957–964.

Cohen, L.J. (2013). The opposite of worry: *The playful parenting approach to childhood anxieties and fears*. New York: Ballantine Books.

Connolly, S.D., & Bernstein, G.A. (2007). Practice parameter for the assessment and treatment of children and adolescents with anxiety disorders. *Journal of the American Academy for Child and Adolescent Psychiatry*, 46:267–283.

Drewes, A. (Ed.) (2009) *Blending play therapy with cognitive-behavioral therapy: Evidence-based and other effective treatments and techniques*. Hoboken, NJ: Wiley.

Dyson, P. (2011). Feelings ring toss. In L. Lowenstein (Ed.), *Assessment and treatment activities for children, adolescents, and families. Vol. 3. Practitioners share their most effective techniques* (pp. 51–53). Toronto, ON: Champion Press.

Eltz, M.J., Shirk, S.R., & Sarlin, N. (1995). Alliance formation and treatment outcome among maltreated adolescents. *Child Abuse & Neglect*, 19:419–431.

Foxman, P. (2004). The worried child: *Recognizing anxiety in children and helping them heal*. Alameda, CA: Hunter House Publishers.

Friedberg, R.D., Crosby, L.E., Friedberg, B.A., Rutter, J.G., & Knight, K.R. (2000). *Making cognitive behavior therapy user-friendly for children. Cognitive and Behavioral Practice*, 6:189–200.

Friedberg, R.D., McClure, J.M., & Garcia, J.H. (2009). *Cognitive therapy techniques for children and adolescents: Tools for enhancing practice*. New York: Guilford Press.

Friedberg, R.D. & McClure, J.M. (2015). *Clinical practice of cognitive therapy with children and adolescents: The nuts and bolts*. New York: Guilford Press.

Gil, E. (2014). *Play in family therapy* (2nd ed.). New York: Guilford Press.

Goodyear-Brown, P. (2002). *Digging for buried treasure: 52 prop-based play therapy interventions for treating the problems of childhood.* Available at www.nurturehouse.org.

Goodyear-Brown, P. (2010). *The worry wars: An anxiety workbook for kids and their helpful adults.* Available at www.nurturehouse.org.

Grant, R.J. (2014). *More play based interventions for autism, ADHD, neurodevelopmental disorders, and developmental disabilities.* RJG Publishing.

Hembree, E.A., Rauch, S.A.M., & Foa, E.B. (2003). Beyond the manual: The insider's guide to prolonged exposure to PTSD. *Cognitive and Behavioral Practice,* 10:22–30.

Kearney, C.A., Wechsler, A., Kauer, H., & Lemos-Miller, A. (2010). Posttraumatic stress disorder in maltreated youth: A review of contemporary research and thought. *Clinical Child and Family Psychology Review,* 13:46–76.

Kendall, P.C., & Beidas, R. S. (2007). Smoothing the trail for dissemination of evidence-based practices for youth: Flexibility within fidelity. *Professional Psychology: Research and Practice,* 38, 13-19.

Kenney-Noziska, S. (2008). *Techniques – techniques – techniques: Play-based activities for children, adolescents, and families.* West Conshohocken, PA: Infinity Publishing.

Killough McGuire, D. & McGuire, D.E. (2001). *Linking parents to play therapy.* New York: Brunner-Routledge.

Knell, S.M. (1993). *Cognitive-behavioral play therapy.* Northvale, NJ: Jason Aronson.

Knell, S.M., & Dasari, M. (2006). Cognitive behavioral play therapy for children with anxiety and phobias. In H.G. Kaduson & C.E. Schaefer (Eds.), *Short-term therapies with children* (2nd ed., pp. 22–50). New York: Guilford Press.

Knell, S.M., & Dasari, M. (2011). *Cognitive-behavioral play therapy.* In S.W. Russ & L.N. Niec (Eds.), *Play in clinical practice: Evidence-based approaches* (pp. 236–262). New York: Guilford Press.

Lamb-Shapiro, J. (2000). *The hyena who lost her laugh: A story about negative thinking.* Melville, NY: Guidance Group.

Lowenstein, L. (1999). *Creative interventions for troubled children and youth.* Toronto, ON: Champion Press.

Lowenstein, L. (2002). *More creative interventions for troubled children and youth.* Toronto, ON: Champion Press.

Lowenstein, L. (Ed.). (2008). *Assessment and treatment activities for children, adolescents, and families: Practitioners share their most effective techniques.* Toronto, ON: Champion Press.

Lowenstein, L. (Ed.). (2010a). *Assessment and treatment activities for children, adolescents, and families. Vol. 2. Practitioners share their most effective techniques.* Toronto, ON: Champion Press.

Lowenstein, L. (Ed.). (2010b). *Creative family therapy techniques: Play, art, and expressive activities to engage children in family sessions.* Toronto, ON: Champion Press.

Lowenstein, L. (Ed.). (2011). *Assessment and treatment activities for children, adolescents, and families. Vol. 3. Practitioners share their most effective techniques.* Toronto, ON: Champion Press.

Manassis, K. (2009). *Cognitive behavioral therapy with children: A guide for the community practitioner.* New York: Routledge.

Matlow, L. (2011). *Thinking about thoughts.* Toronto.

Ormhaug, S.M., Jensen, T.K., Wentzel-Larsen, T., & Shirk, S.R. (2013). The therapeutic alliance in treatment of traumatized youths: Relation to outcome in a randomized clinical trial. *Journal of Consulting and Clinical Psychology, 47*:225–240.

Pincus, D.B, Chase, R.M., Chow C., Weiner C.L., and Pian, J. (2011). Integrating play into cognitive-behavioral therapy for child anxiety disorders. In S.W. Russ & L.N. Niec (Eds.), *Play in clinical practice: Evidence-based approaches* (pp. 218–235). New York: Guilford Press.

Pincus, D. (2012). *Growing up brave.* New York: Little, Brown and Company.

Piper, W. (1930). *The little engine that could.* New York: Platt & Munk.

Plummer, D.M. (2012). *Focusing and calming games for children: Mindfulness strategies and activities to help children relax, concentrate, and take control.* London: Jessica Kingsley Publishers.

Podell, J.L., Martin, E.D., & Kendall, P.C. (2009). Incorporating play within a manual-based treatment for children and adolescents with anxiety disorders. In A.A. Drewes (Ed.), *Blending play therapy with cognitive behavioral therapy: Evidence-based and other effective treatments and techniques* (pp. 165–178). Hoboken, NJ: Wiley.

Podell, J.L., Mychailyszyn, M., Edmunds, J., Puleo, C.M., & Kendall, P.C. (2010). The Coping Cat program for anxious youth: The FEAR plan comes to life. *Cognitive and Behavioral Practice, 17*:132–141.

Schaefer, C.E. & Drewes, A. (2013). *The therapeutic powers of play: 20 core agents of change* (2nd ed.). Hoboken, NJ: Wiley.

Shelby, J.S. & Berk, M.S. (2009). Play therapy, pedagogy, and CBT: An argument for interdisciplinary synthesis. In A.A. Drewes (Ed.), *Blending play therapy with cognitive behavioral therapy: Evidence-based and other effective treatments and techniques* (pp. 17–40). Hoboken, NJ: Wiley.

Schneider, S., Blatter-Meunier, J., Herren, C., In-Albon, T., Adornetto, C., Meyer, A., & Lavallee, K.L. (2013). The efficacy of a family-based cognitive-behavioral treatment for separation anxiety disorder in children aged 8–13: A randomized comparison with a general anxiety program. *Journal of Consulting and Clinical Psychology* 81(5):932–940.

Sousa, B. (2011). Google it. In L. Lowenstein (Ed.), *Assessment and treatment activities for children, adolescents, and families. Vol. 3. Practitioners share their most effective techniques* (pp. 2–3). Toronto, ON: Champion Press.

Spence, S.H., Donovan, C., & Brechman-Toussaint, M. (2000). The treatment of childhood social phobia: The effectiveness of a social skills training-based, cognitive-behavioural intervention, with and without parental involvement. *Journal of Child Psychology and Psychiatry* 41:713–726.

Stallard, P. (2005). *A clinician's guide to think good-feel good: Using CBT with children and young people.* Chichester, UK: Wiley.

Springer, C.I., & Misurell, J.R. (2015). *Game-based cognitive-behavioral therapy for child sexual abuse.* New York: Springer.

Van Hollander, T. (2011). Mancala feeling stones. In L. Lowenstein (Ed.), *Assessment and treatment activities for children, adolescents, and families. Vol. 3. Practitioners share their most effective techniques* (pp. 60–61). Toronto, ON: Champion Press.

Velting, O.N., Setzer, N.J., & Albano, A.M. (2004). Update on and advances in assessment and cognitive-behavioral treatment of anxiety disorders in children and adolescents, *Professional Psychology: Research and Practice* 42:42–54.

Wagner, A.P. (2005). *Worried no more: Help and hope for anxious children.* (2nd ed.). Rochester, NY: Lighthouse Press.

Wagner, A. P. (2013). *Worried no more: Teaching Tools and Forms on CD.* (3rd ed.). Apex, NC: Lighthouse Press.

Wilson, R., & Lyons, L. (2013). *Anxious kids, anxious parents: 7 ways to stop the worry cycle and raise courageous and independent children.* Deerfield Beach, FL: Health Communications Inc.

Zucker, B. (2009). *Anxiety-free kids: An interactive guide for parents and children.* Waco, TX: Prufrock Press, Inc.

Organizations

Anxiety and Mental Health

Anxiety and Depression Association of America: www.adaa.org

Anxiety Disorders Association of Canada: www.anxietycanada.ca

Anxiety Wellness Center: www.anxietywellness.com

Child Anxiety Network: www.childanxiety.net

National Alliance on Mental Illness: www.nami.org

National Institute of Mental Health: www.nimh.nih.gov

Worry Wise Kids: www.worrywisekids.org

Cognitive-Behavioral Therapy

Academy of Cognitive Therapy: www.academyofct.org

Association for Behavioral and Cognitive Therapies: www.abct.org

Canadian Association of Cognitive and Behavioural Therapies: www.cacbt.ca

European Association for Behavioral and Cognitive Therapies: www.eabct.eu

International Association for Cognitive Psychotherapy: www.the-iacp.com

Play Therapy

Association for Play Therapy: www.a4pt.org

British Association of Play Therapists: www.bapt.info

Canadian Association for Child and Play Therapy: www.cacpt.com

Play Therapy International: www.playtherapy.org

Australasia Pacific Play Therapy Association: www.appta.org.au